Louis I. Kahn Visiting As

cultural cues

cu

cu

cu

al cu

Joe Day

ltural

cues

Tom Wiscombe

cul

ural cult

Adib Cúre &
Carie Penabad

cues

Yale School of Architecture

Yale School of Architecture
180 York Street
New Haven, Connecticut 06520
www.architecture.yale.edu

Distributed by ActarD
355 Lexington Avenue, 8th floor
New York, NY 10017
www.actar-d.com

This book was made possible through
an endowment for the Louis I. Kahn
Visiting Assistant Professorship at
the Yale School of Architecture. It is
the sixth in a series of publica-
tions of the Louis I. Kahn Assistant
Professorship published through the
dean's office.

Editors: Nina Rappaport and
Jeffrey M. Pollack
Design: MGMT. design

Library of Congress Control Number:
2015934481

ISBN 978-1-9402916-0-4 (pbk.)

Louis I. Kahn Visiting Assistant Professorship

The Louis I. Kahn Visiting Assistant Professorship is Yale's second endowed chair to honor the architect. Established in 2004, the professorship brings to the school younger architects who practice and teach, offering them the opportunity to lead advanced design studios and seminars. The Kahn Visiting Assistant Professorship carries with it the expectation that the work of the visiting professors and their students will be published so that others may benefit from the ideas developed and exchanged in the studios and seminars.

Louis I. Kahn (1901–74), perhaps the greatest American architect of the post-World War II era, was closely associated with Yale as a teacher and practicing architect. Yale is home to his first important building, the extension to the Art Gallery (1951–53), and his last, the Center for British Art (1969–77). Kahn was fresh to teaching when he came to Yale, in 1947, to begin what would be ten years as chief critic in the architecture school. As a teacher, he worked closely with students encouraging them to go beyond their initial ideas about architecture, as he himself was trying to go beyond his own ideas. Kahn inspired a generation of architects, leading them to new insights that became the basis of their independent work.

Twenty-four studios have been offered by Louis I. Kahn Visiting Assistant Professors, beginning with Gregg Pasquarelli, whose studio—along with that of successor appointees, Galia Solomonoff and Mario Gooden—was published in the book *Layered Urbanisms*, in 2007. The studios of the next three appointees to the chair, Jeanne Gang, Sunil Bald, and Mark Tsurumaki, were documented in *Negotiated Terrains*, in 2009. The studio led by FAT Architects—Sean Griffiths, Sam Jacob, and Charles Holland—collaborating with Edward P. Bass Visiting Fellow developer Nick Johnson of Urban Splash, was published in *Urban Integration/ Bishopsgate Goods Yard*, in 2010. The studios of Christopher Sharples, William Sharples, and Ali Rahim were published in the volume *Turbulence*, in 2011. *Architecture Inserted*, published in 2012, presented the work and studios of Eric Bunge and Mimi Hoang, Chris Perry, and Liza Fior with Katherine Clarke. The previous volume, *Renewing Architectural Typologies*, published in 2013, documented the work and studios of Makram El Kadi and Ziad Jamaleddine of L.E.F.T., Tom Coward, Daisy Froud, Vincent Lacovara, Geoff Shearcroft of AOC, and Hernán Díaz Alonso.

This volume, *Cultural Cues*, presenting the studios of Joe Day of Deegan Day Design, Tom Wiscombe of Tom Wiscombe Architecture, and Adib Cúre and Carie Penabad of Cúre & Penabad, reflects, as do its predecessors, Yale's studio pedagogy, which is founded on the bedrock of a diverse approach toward architecture and independent thinking.

Introduction—Nina Rappaport & Jeffrey M. Pollack

Cultural Cues is the sixth book to feature the work of the Louis I. Kahn Visiting Assistant Professorship and that of the advanced studios at the Yale School of Architecture.

This book includes the research and designs that emerged from studios taught at Yale by Joe Day of the Los Angeles–based architectural practice Deegan Day Design, Tom Wiscombe of the Los Angeles–based practice Tom Wiscombe Architecture, and Adib Cúre and Carie Penabad of the Miami-based practice Cúre & Penabad. By reexamining the cultural fixtures of the cinema, the museum, and the house, along with their greater context, the projects offer contemporary architectural responses to the cues of the city at large.

Joe Day explores how filmic sensibilities can inform architectural design. Beginning by analyzing film to learn new ways to manipulate space, perspective, and narrative, the studio challenges conventional notions of media and how it is consumed while bringing the context of the city into the heart of the exploration.

Tom Wiscombe investigates new methods of digital design and their role in the constantly evolving architectural discourse. By testing strategies of wrapping objects within objects and negotiating the stretching of a building's outer skin on a Schaulager-type museum, the studio projects exhibit powerful figural explorations.

Adib Cúre and Carie Penabad examine the current condition of urbanism and housing in Central Havana, Cuba, in relation to other urban conditions worldwide. Following extensive analysis of the role of housing in the city, the culture of Cuba, and Central Havana itself, the studio attempts to find innovative solutions to the need for housing in an already extremely dense setting.

Each section of the book begins with an interview with the architects about the work of their firm. The essays and project briefs framing the studio explorations introduce the research and design strategies, providing insight into the pedagogical approach of these practitioner-educators and proposing new ways to interpret the cultural fixtures of the city.

The editors would like to thank the professors and the students for helping to make this document possible. From Joe Day's studio, we would like to thank Amir Mikhaeil, Lauren Chapman, Ilsa Falis, Danielle Duryea, Michael Holborn, Will Fox, Christos Bolos, Lang Wang, and Amy DeDonato. From Tom Wiscombe's studio, we would like to thank Sarah Gill, Teoman Ayas, Peter Logan, Lauren Page, Dino Kiratzidis, Jacqueline Ho, Jing Liu, and Sierra Cobb. From Adib Cúre and Carie Penabad's studio, we would like to thank Alexander Chabla, Edward Hsu, Antonia Devine, Mansi Maheshwari, Alexander Osei-Bonsu, Lauren Page, Christina Argyros, Jeffrey Pollack, Katharine Storr, and Jeongyeap Shin. Special recognition is due to Amy DeDonato and Jacqueline Ho for their editorial work on their respective studio sections.

We extend our utmost appreciation to Sarah Gephart and Federico Pérez Villoro of MGMT. design, copy editor David Delp, proof reader Judith Beck, and Dean Robert A. M. Stern. We hope this volume presents new possibilities for architectural exploration and elicits debate on the future of design.

01—Joe Day, NOWplex

Interview with Joe Day

Joe Day discussed his work and his teaching with Nina Rappaport, prior to the beginning of the Yale studio.

Nina Rappaport: In "After Ecologies," your introduction to the new edition of Reyner Banham's *Four Ecologies*, you talk about how his perspective of the city shaped following generations. How has his work specifically influenced yours?

Joe Day: Banham's first contribution to my life was the site for my senior thesis as a Yale undergrad. I was trying to imagine Los Angeles from New Haven when my thesis adviser, Patrick Pinnell, suggested I try Banham's *Four Ecologies*. I used his beautiful aerial shot of the 10-405 Freeway cloverleaf as a site for a parabolic prison that hovered over the connecting ramps, making commuters overseers. The role of Banham's writing in my life since then is hard for me to circumscribe. Banham found a way to write within the discipline with an incredible elasticity, as Sylvia Lavin puts it, and I think that sense of testing the envelope of what can be, in fact, architecture, seeing what the discipline can actually absorb, is really central for me. My work often involves a specific interplay between art and architecture, but I don't aspire to be an artist. The often unseemly ways that architecture, art, and popular culture commingle in Los Angeles but remain culturally distinct was probably supported as much by the legacy of the Independent Group and Banham's sensibility as by anything native. We named our son after Banham, but, true to his informality, we borrowed his first name, not his last.

Your 2013 book, *Corrections and Collections: Architectures for Art and Crime*, parallels the typologies of prisons and museums. While one could say they are both fortress like and heterotopic, what are the more political and formal ideas you intend to provoke by discussing them in the same breath? And how have these ideas informed urban development?

The first course I taught at Sci-Arc was with urban historian Mike Davis, and it was a survey of the California prison system—we toured over twenty institutions. This built upon interests I had developed while working on my undergraduate thesis. However, my graduate studies focused on artists and museums, in particular the Matta family: Roberto Matta, the Surrealist painter, and Gordon Matta-Clark. (I was lucky enough to meet Gordon's mother, Anne Clark, just before she passed away.) Both artists had a highly charged relationship to architecture and museums, and the Mattas were very interested in Piranesi and his "Carceri" series. So I found myself oscillating back and forth between these two subjects. *Corrections and Collections* builds out of a thesis that these two building types are paradigmatic in their staging of "scopic" relationships between viewer and viewed and their elevation of visual economies to architectural absolutes.

How do these prototypes relate to the development of cities and the economic value of land and space? With museums we have seen the Bilbao effect, for example . . . but prisons?

What I stumbled upon in the late 1980s and early 1990s was that both building types were playing an interestingly complementary role in American urban renewal in terms of the way they shore up urban areas. Jails have a far less dramatic but equally powerful role in the sense that, for every cell you add, the number of civil-sector employees in the city, courthouses, and custodial staff multiplies.

How have surveillance and prison systems played a part in cities and infiltrated into your own work in interpreting the urban design of cities?

I think both prisons and museums have had a strangely disproportionate role in the polarized way we discuss American urban space and how we use it. In *Corrections and Collections*, I try to pull the conversations back to architecture and design. It begins with an odd aesthetic convergence in Minimalism, with the "penitential modern" terms that Ada Louise Huxtable used to describe the Hirshhorn Museum.

Many people think it looks like a bunker or a spaceship with a doughnut hole.

In some ways, that subtle strangeness interests me more. That convergence gave me a place to start—and Kahn is also a major figure there. In the 1980s and early 1990s, the early stages of both building booms paralleled what was being discussed in the schools. Foucault and, more generally, Institutional Critique play out in some interesting ways and stir innovation in both building types—strikingly so in prisons but also in museums. The all-in-one spatial models of the Panopticon and the Guggenheim drive a lot of Post-Modern examples. Then, I think things shift around the millennium from Minimal and Post-Minimalist questions of objects and bodies in space into the production of total, immersive environments. In both prisons and museums we started to build these encyclopedic institutions—enormous urban jails to serve the huge networks that we have built. With renovations to the Metropolitan Museum of Art and LACMA, among others, the game of museum expansion shifted into an urban scale and to questions of territory as form.

As an architect practicing in Los Angeles—working mostly on

small-scale houses, installations, shops, and showrooms as well as museums—what is your approach as it relates to your writings and research?

I returned to Los Angeles in 1990 out of a real passion for L.A. Modern architecture, which seems a pretty anachronistic reason now. My first job there was working with Frank Israel on his book, and I felt vested in that dialogue. I am working on two houses, C-Glass and 4/Way House, that have been built slowly, and I see them as exercises to either side of the Neutra and Schindler divide in L.A. Modernism. My interest in visual economies plays out in some surprising ways in the Los Angeles domestic scale, where voyeurism and exhibitionism are less verboten. The small-scale and the conceptual project converge in my teaching through cinema. I feel that cinema is the third leg of this institutional argument as well as a guiding principle for how spaces are understood and generated

in Los Angeles and, certainly, how people choose to frame their lives there.

So, the Columbia College Hollywood film school project is a really fortuitous opportunity for you?

The fifty-year-old film school now occupies the old Panavision Camera Building, in Tarzana. Their promise is that, within fifteen minutes of entry, you will get a camera in your hands. Every corner of the school was themed with places for students to shoot in, and they realized that they hadn't left any space for viewing what they were producing.

What are your main concepts for the space? I see a number of little stacked theaters and gathering spaces.

We have very little space to work with, so, in order to get a sense of how much screening area we could

provide, we took the corners of light-projection cones and ran them through the space as vectors. We ended up with this odd argyle pattern from four points of projection. They are spatially efficient, but, because of the irregularities of the space, we were able to set up some as closed black-box conditions and let others bleed together as exhibition space. Early on, we imagined fortified pan-optic projection rooms but realized two months into the project that, with digital projectors, that kind of centricity and fortification just wasn't necessary anymore. It's a modest discovery, but it opened up the project.

How has your experiment with exhibit design, *Blow x Blow*, at SCI-Arc, influenced the college project? How have you expanded beyond what you had imagined?

It allowed us to prototype some of the ideas. These smaller, faster projects let us go back into those initial techniques. Because it has to do with filmic experience, the role of the script is interesting to us at a literal level, along with the degree of sophistication that you can bring to scripting now. Rather than use the four edges of the cone of projection that bounces through the space and establish baseline conditions, we controlled vector length but randomized their direction. The most useful scripting in this project had to do with the way it is structured. Plexiglas fins transect a translucent white honeycomb material, giving it the rigidity to span the space.

In your C-Glass House, one can see Modernist aspects, both in its positioning and materials. How have you used that as a base to go forward?

Our client worked on a Mies retrospective, so she was very aware of what a glass house could be, but the Case Study Houses and many recent glass pavilions by artists compounded the whole question of how you can build a glass enclosure. Dan Graham's glass pavilions and Craig Ellwood's crystalline houses in the 1950s were important "lenses" for me, as I had experienced those, rather than Mies'

01

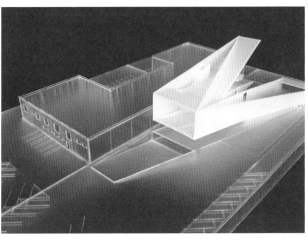

02

(01) C-Glass House, Marin, California (02) Center for Contemporary Cinema, Tarzana, California

Interview with Joe Day

04

WILL
CALL

94   95

(03) *Blow x Blow* installation

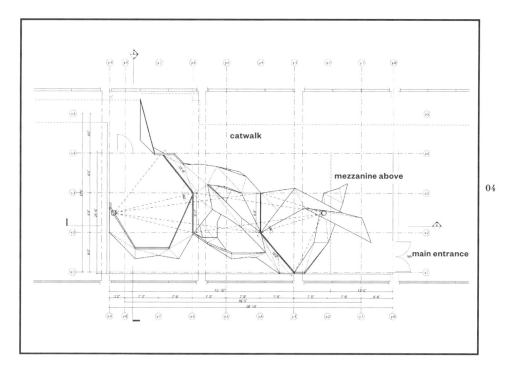

(04) *Blow x Blow* plan

or Johnson's. But when I start with all these citations, I may have buried this little building.

The C-Glass House is about engagement with an epic landscape, not only in terms of its scenographic view but also in terms of its stance toward the elements. The site gets 100-mile-an-hour winds in opposite directions, so quite a bit of engineering, for the frame as well as the inset and overlay glazing systems, went into accounting for those lateral loads without building a huge cage. It is translucent on the land side and transparent on the water side, and there is now a square lawn on the ocean side of the house, thanks to Dean Stern, who said that until there is grass in the foreground, we don't have a glass house to talk about.

Lot 49, another small house, in Topanga, biases toward a narrower ocean view, through more complicated topography and circumstances. Here, geology and fire threat—and Pynchonesque paranoia about both—dictate many terms of engagement. The floors of the house are staggered up a steep ridge, with a zinc-clad "fire blanket" draping over the whole. Covered parking is required for fire safety, so, in this case, we designed a carport that rotates 90 degrees up and becomes a screen for the living room.

How did your clothing line, Dayware, evolve from an interest

in architectural production and fabrication techniques to assembling garments using patterns and templates?

My interest in triangulation and facetry in building envelopes began with clothing. A pattern in clothing allows you to create curvature and seams through a garment but also allows you to see it in total, at once. But the basic idea driving Dayware was really prosaic, as it is more of a clothing than a fashion project: my interest was in making workwear for artists and architects. I developed a grid of garments that I thought took care of most of my basic needs. My coat here is probably the most complicated Dayware piece. It shows my interest in how interior and exterior surfaces meet, where you are forced to make sense of silhouette and drape in the outer envelope of a garment through its edge conditions and detailing, then dealing with all of the questions that come up in interiors—garment or architecture—at a micro scale.

What was the theme of your studio, and what were you hoping the students would produce?

The program is a center for cinema, which is as close as I get to church these days and about as phenomenologically inclined as I will ever get. I see this as an antidote to the museum

and the prison or an escape from that dyad into, again, a more triangulated field. The more specific and strategic architecture is around visual relationships, the more effective it is, not only in terms of creating or reanimating urban space but of actually generating discipline-changing architecture. In certain respects, the cinema is an overlooked paradigm in that discussion. I see this as something that should occupy our cultural landscape as much as LACMA and MOCA.

Will it be a museum, a place to show film, or mainly for events?

I think that will vary according to the decisions students choose to make. They will take a strong curatorial role and, I hope, be broad in their ambitions. I'd like to believe it could be an effective, and even definitive, museum of cinema. I worry that the expectations of a museum can be incredibly stultifying, and I hope it has more the dynamic of a Kunsthalle in some ways. Right now, there isn't anywhere to see film in a radical gradient of film production, from studio work to YouTube outtakes to art. That is why I was interested in teaching this studio here and now.

"So, Why Triangles?"—Joe Day & Michelle Paul

Emmanuel Petit asked this disarmingly simple question, "Why triangles?" after my lecture at the Yale School of Architecture.

I would spend the rest of the semester marshalling a convincing response. The lecture was titled "DELTASCOPES" and explored my fascination with projection and the many forms of cultural production that depend on it: drawing methods, filmmaking, urban expansion, utopian speculation. "Delta" translates from the Greek as both "change" and "triangulation" and seemed, when combined with the less ambiguous term scope, to corral my brokerage between vision and architecture in a useful way. I had been warned, though, against inventing a lecture title out of amalgamated terms and to expect a sniper's accuracy in the questions that would follow the slides.

As for the preponderance of three-sided figures, I had a few answers for Petit but could hear them ringing hollow that night: Triangles create efficient surfaces without curves (and curvature, in my generation, is a career-defining choice); cones of projection are, in fact, pyramidal combinations of triangles; I even alluded to Bill Clinton's notion of political triangulation. "DELTASCOPES" presented a host of projects, diagrams, and quotations that found common cause, if not precisely developmental progress, in a shared geometric motif. The talk did "triangulate" between design, criticism, and analysis but only hinted at a deeper, generative trigonometry that was building from project to project. If the choreography of vision through architecture depends on how one locates and modulates the "open triangle" of a viewer's cone of vision, the designs included in my lecture registered that correspondence in many ways but not yet with a firm sense of purpose.

Pattern, Perspective, Projection

The "Petit Challenge," as it resonated through the spring, was not a small matter to me. The topic of the studio NOWplex that I would teach with Michelle Paul and the priorities of my design practice, Deegan-Day Design, are closely linked. Almost all projects at DDDllc begin with a discussion of projection. In many, there are instances of actual projected imagery, but, in most, the issue takes a less direct, more nuanced form: How will specific issues and demands be met through projective techniques? How will the design project the client's ambitions? How, in the end, will the word *project* come to be understood as both a noun and a verb?

The linkage between projection and triangulation is a contested one within our field. The conventions of orthographic projection, in which lines run in a constant perpendicular or parallel, yields little or no obligatory triangulation. The most charged discussions of projection in contemporary architecture, from the neo-Cubism of the New York Five through Robin Evan's parsing of descriptive geometries in The Projective Cast and on to the conjoining of projection and shape by Robert Somol and Sarah Whiting, all downplay perspectival or filmic projection, emanating from single points of origin, in favor of the isometric method of parallel extrusion and translation that are dear to designers and builders. However, most modes of conventional representation yield triangulation at every turn—lines diminishing to vanishing points, the splay and pinch of orthogonal volumes seen from any single point of view.

In both perspective and cinema, all these oblique lines result from a visual field that presumes, and privileges, hierarchies of sight and location. I come to my interest in scopic properties via a more general one in architecture and power relations. A defining triangle in my intellectual life links the three most visually predetermined building types: the prison, the museum, and the cinema. As I was preparing to teach at Yale, I was also in the final throes of completing a book, *Corrections and Collections: Architectures for Art and Crime* (Routledge, 2013), which explores the concurrent museum and prison booms since Minimalism. Both of those building types rely on lines of sight to establish regimens of control through fortified enclosures; both have recently experienced periods of unprecedented transformation in the service of an ever-expanding range of transgressions and transgressors. At Yale, though, I was eager for a reprieve from those two relatively stolid institutions and eager for a foray into my third and favorite architecture defined almost solely by its visual parameters, the movie theater. The "NOW" in NOWplex stood for "north of Wilshire" but also for what I wanted to be doing right then and there, which was something other than finishing my book!

I am interested foremost in how architecture orchestrates vision and how design may act as a crucial intermediate condition in any scopic equation. If "visuality," or the social construction of vision, begins with the roles of viewer and viewed, we ask what separates them, and what makes them legible to one another?

Dayware, a line of workwear for artists that I developed in the late 1990s, answered that question rather directly with clothing that was/is a fast, variable screening device between parties: The wearer projects his or her desired identity—who, I wondered in my twenties, wouldn't want to be seen as an artist?—and a beholder projects validation or skepticism accordingly. Perhaps my central fascination with Dayware, though, lies in the device of the pattern, the specific shapes of cut fabric that are combined to create a garment. This is the DNA of the clothing industry, blueprints but more so, as they are enacted at 1-to-1 scale. However, depending on which textile is used and how edges are joined—how a pattern is read and interpreted during sourcing and production—a single collection of flat shapes can generate a nearly infinite series of expressions.

With its fast turnaround, Dayware was also an antidote to the often glacial pace of architectural production. At the turn of 2000, we began two residential projects on undeveloped coastal lots, both of which, due to cost, approvals, and the vicissitudes of construction on remote sites, would take more than a decade to complete. In each, filmic projection plays a defining role: At the 4/Way House in Topanga, California, a carport tilts up ninety degrees to become a screen for the main house; in Marin, the scenographic presence of the C-Glass House is meant to invoke Mies, Johnson, and even the Casa Malaparte in Godard's *Contempt*, all favorites of the client. The slow migration toward building permitting for both homes paralleled my studio's adoption of more advanced digital design tools and afforded me the time to diagnose some of my core interests in the staging and framing of architectural experience. As different as the C-Glass House and 4/Way House look, both were resolved through a common design process that cycled through questions of perspective, pattern, and projection. Both houses orient toward remarkable coastal views from large, open parcels; the siting and stance of each involved a complex on-site mix of compasses, cameras, transits, framing poles, and spooled measuring lines simply to direct and quantify the views that each home would eventually enjoy. These in situ notations resulted in perspective views resembling the "Non-Site" descriptions of Robert Smithson. Patterns were gradually developed for the envelopes of both homes: in Marin, one of alternating transparent and translucent banding to modulate a sweeping ocean view, and, in Topanga in the 4/Way House, one of fitted, directional surfaces and apertures that tease out the intensities of its setting—a diving, sawtooth topography reminiscent of David Hockney's wavy *Mulholland Drive*.

Methods of projection factor into both the perspective analysis and pattern work of both designs but developed more independently in the structural resolution of each. In C-Glass, the steel frame of the house was engineered as a series of diminishing cantilevered projections, beginning with its eight vertical posts and caissons, sized to withstand 100-mile-an-hour winds blowing in alternating directions and concluding in a series

of localized projections to support the balcony, shade, and the five-foot offset of the front elevation. Two truss profiles in two orientations rotate and stagger across the length of the 4/Way House, determining both its silhouette and its tent like interior. The architectural projection of these profiles through the house and carport structures is countered by an actual filmic projection between them: The tilt-up carport becomes a movie screen when viewed from the house above. In the gradually expanding wake of these two houses, our work became more specifically tied to cinema in the ongoing Media Center for Columbia College Hollywood and in *Blow x Blow*, an installation in the SCI-Arc Gallery, in 2009. Both these designs began with governing cones of projection and reception that were themselves optimized for viewing quality and occupancy. In CCH's Media Center, the vectoral edges of cones of projection were allowed to "bounce" through the available space, generating a sort of 3-D honeycomb lattice or argyle pattern that, in turn, yielded a network of screening spaces. In *Blow x Blow*, project designer Yo Oshima developed a script by which a randomized braid of projected vectors passed through the gallery to reinforce a back-to-back diptych of translucent screens. Artists Andrea Fraser, An Te Liu, and Josh Melnick exhibited their work in quadrilateral projection. The installation was later repurposed for Paul Young Projects, a gallery specializing in new media art.

More recently, we have explored other, more literal deployments of projection parameters in competitions for new cultural spaces in Chicago and London and, returning to our residential roots, in a proposal for a studio addition for photographer and filmmaker Tao Ruspoli. The Chicago competition required proposals to fill an eighty-foot cylindrical void left vacant by a stalled tower development. In its place, we proposed a "total cinema" that, like Walter Gropius' Total Theater of 1927, would rotate in its seating between performative configurations, forming a cinema-in-the-round below grade and an IMAX housed in a windsock above. For the London Cinema

01

"So, Why Triangles?"—Joe Day & Michelle Paul

(02/03/04) C-Glass House, Marin, California

01—Joe Day, NOWplex —The Essay—pp. 16–17

(05) 4/Way House, Topanga, California

Challenge, twenty randomized cones of projection were "Boolean-ed" or subtracted from a solidified volume of the site constraints to create new orders of cinematic interiority and cross-penetration. In the recent addition, the specific aspect ratios of still photography (4 × 5, 8 × 10 inches) govern all proportions in plan, while screen formats—16:9 for IMAX—determine sectional relationships and the "aperture" sizes of windows and doors.

The invitation to teach at Yale allowed me to shift from a preoccupation with the mechanics of filmic exhibition to an exploration of how cinema and architecture, as distinct and ascendant twentieth-century disciplines, could feed off of one another's discoveries. The studio that I led at Yale with Michelle Paul, NOWplex: A Center for Contemporary Cinema, tackled the space of the moving image as well as the urban and representational questions attendant to both cinema and architecture.

We began with a few introductory exercises designed to bring a "filmic" sensibility to the semester's work, especially methods of projection and perspective. Students employed traditional drawing techniques, diagramming, and animated motion graphics to analyze specific films, and most chose rather high-brow auteurs to examine: Alfred Hitchcock, Stanley Kubrick, Kar Wai Wong, Andrei Tarkovsky, Jean-Luc Godard, P. T. Anderson, Michelangelo Antonioni, Gonzalo López-Gallego, Jørgen Leth, and David Lynch. The close examination of the physical and implied space, pacing, and rhythm, as well as the editorial and narrative structures built by these directors, carried through the semester.

A second exercise, the analysis of planar dissections—geometric patterns that bridge between primary shapes—became a way for some students to discover and claim formal territory. These exercises also provided an introductory exploration of scripting with Grasshopper as the students multiplied, manipulated, and made their own 3-D manifold networks. They 3-D-printed these explorations and brought them to Los Angeles, where, during the study trip to SCI-Arc, the projects were reviewed by a jury of three previous Yale Louis I. Kahn Assistant Professors:

Hernan Diaz-Alonso, Tom Wiscombe, and Marcelo Spina.

Once in L.A., the students revealed their various Sun Belt pedigrees (Texas, Utah, and three from Florida) and received immediate vehicle upgrades to a red convertible Mustang and an extended Jeep. The trip was an Angeleno juxtaposition of old and new, or of then, now, and the future. Students stayed in downtown L.A., two blocks from Gehry's Disney Hall and Morphosis' Caltrans building. Highlights included a tour with Ming Fung and Craig Hodgetts of their renovated historic Egyptian Theater, a tour of Gehry Partners, a visit to Moss' Culver City, and a trip to La Jolla to view the Salk Institute. At Paul Young Projects, a gallery specializing in video art, Paul Young presented his eye-opening, immersive, and defining look at what contemporary film is today and how it can be amplified by physical space.

After a midterm review, when the various directions of research were just beginning to cross-pollinate in most projects, students were able to reach resolution in their final projects. The most successful projects rose to the challenge of cinematic speculation, both in terms of generating new kinds of space to host new media and applying cinematic principles to design in novel ways. Their conjecture addressed a current and future world of moving images, one less bound by conventions of closed theaters and redundant multiplexes and more open to new habits of public and private viewing and recognizing the rise of interactive participation, rather than passive consumption.

The studio entertained a trio of thematic directions, or "scenes," that were explored by the projects, each of which capitalized on a distinct set of relationships between architecture and filmmaking. In the "filmic" concept, emphasis fell on specific parallels between architecture's and cinema's respective media and authorship, parallels the students discovered through close analysis of a director's work and a transposition of those findings into spatial sequences. In the "typological" projects, the conventions of the cinema as building type were reconfigured, reinterpreted, or redistributed in site-specific ways.

Finally, in the "technical" series, specific methods and parameters of making or presenting films are radically repurposed toward architectonic ends.

The first three filmic projects reflect deeply on the evolving roles of the architect and the director as well as the increasingly dispersed modes of authorship that each deploys in the sequencing of time and space through their chosen medium. In Amir Mikhaeil's project, "Time-Image," which received the Feldman Award, a series of cinematic encounters, based on the nested temporalities portrayed by Tarkovsky, gives rise to a torqued volume cleverly and dramatically attuned to its context. An exemplary project in many respects, "Time-Image" has haunted us most for its cogent distillation of a director's dense, complicated sensibility into a clear, convincing architecture. Lauren Chapman parlayed her fluency with Hitchcock's work (she studied film before architecture) into a head-spinning extrapolation of *Vertigo* within cubic parameters, a proposal she titled "Déjà Vu." And Ilsa Falis developed a series of ambient, intertwined spaces that oscillate between the cool objectivity of Leth's *Perfect Human* and the humid allure of Kar Wai Wong's *In the Mood for Love*.

The next three typological projects hinge on new understandings and deployments of the cinema as building type—understandings and deployments recently liberated in critical respects by the advent of digital projection. Danielle Duryea examined the element of the marquee as an independent and radically malleable volumetric signifier and asked how that marker might be transformed to announce new forms of cinematic experience in new media art and non-linear narratives. Michael Holborn and Will Fox both restaged the relationship between movie-going and auto-centric Los Angeles. In Holborn's project, as in Wright's Guggenheim, the spiral of a parking structure suggests a centripetal multiplex, with projection spaces splaying out from a cylindrical helix as the glow of headlights might rake out from a car ascending a parking ramp. By contrast, Fox dispersed a series of projection spaces in the form of prismatic voids through existing buildings down the length of Wilshire. Like *Conical Intersect*, Gordon Matta-Clark's seminal film of boring into a Parisian apartment complex in 1975, Fox's project suggests that the high vacancy rate in Wilshire's high-rises could be imagined, instead, as opportunities for interface between urban and cultural realms.

Finally, three students took up specific technological attributes of filmmaking and repurposed them to yield architectural outcomes. Christos Bolos produced a thorough, sequenced diagram of spaces that were suited to various film formats and based on their aspect ratios and throw requirements; then, he melded those limit conditions into a faceted screening apparatus above grade and modeled surface of reception below. In perhaps the most radical departure from the brief, Lang Wang made a film in which her cinema proposal evolved as the material residue or backdrop of the cinematic progression she imagined through a series of modeled, inhabitable surfaces. Amy DeDonato produced a stellar array of analytical and generative operations based on the relationship between the script-as-text in film and scripting as a crucial transition between analog and digital methodologies in architecture. DeDonato's series of schemes—she produced at least four NOWplex proposals between the midterm and final reviews—were a tour de force meditation on the limits and paradoxes of authorship, whether by auteur or architect, in the face of digital determinism.

Each of these nine projects met and, in most cases, vastly exceeded our expectations for the NOWplex studio, and each coins a provocative reply to the question, posed at the semester's start, of Emmanuel Petit. Triangles and triangulation abound in these projects—literal, figural and conceptual. The strongest projects capitalized on the fundamental dynamism of filmmaking, especially, as revealed particularly in the so-called director's cut, the escalating mobility of the camera in tracking shots, fades, and other transitions, to imagine new methods of spatial generation and architectonic resolution. More to Petit's point, however, all nine students used the transdisciplinary ambitions of the NOWplex brief to develop unforeseen outcomes by triangulating between film, architecture, and their own preoccupations.

06

07

08

(06/07/08) 4/Way House, Topanga, California

"So, Why Triangles?"—Joe Day & Michelle Paul

(09) 4/Way House, Topanga, California

01—Joe Day, NOWplex —The Essay—pp. 20-21

NOWplex: A Center for Contemporary Cinema

Entering the twenty-first century, architecture and cinema are the two dominant art forms of our time, and the predominant mediums across the arts. Blockbuster films and iconic buildings are the most broadly experienced and widely debated forms of cultural production, equally spectacular, state-of-the-art, and coincident with many technological and sociological levels. Steroidal utopian fantasies arrive in both forms, often with a startling convergence in budget, staffing, scheduling, and software.[1]

On the other hand, the techniques and protocols of cinema and architecture have become the lingua franca for all the visual arts. Work in installation and new media requires not just a practical grasp of building and filmmaking but an increasingly nuanced perspective on the many varieties of disciplinary backfill and erosion that immediately surface when those modes of signification are employed. In his many pavilions and his occasional films, Dan Graham, for example, proves both a more articulate interlocutor of Mies van der Rohe than many architects and a closer follower of Antonioni than most contemporary auteurs.

For all their storied history and personal impact, however, few recent movie theaters rise to the level of compelling architecture. In fact, the contemporary cinematic experience almost always reinforces a broad high-low irony that the least thematically ambitious films enjoy the most heavily engineered screening environments. However, the opposite is true: Advanced projection-based art is almost always witnessed in ad hoc gallery installation.[2]

This studio addressed a variety of the challenges cinema poses for architecture, both in practical terms—by providing new armatures for cinematic experience—and in conceptual terms, by developing new architectonic responses to an increasingly "filmic" contemporary urban condition.

We examined and responded to two strains of environmental projection: the claiming of urban space via branded structures and the ceding of that space to the ambient possibilities of new media. To challenge these tendencies, we repurposed cinematic techniques to spur new orders of spatial and structural sequencing as well as new environments for engaging with new art.

Neither a multiplex nor a museum, the new Center for Contemporary Cinema capitalized on aspects of both in pursuit of a novel cultural and spatial formation: NOWplex. The past two decades have brought major advances in both visual technologies and in the theorizing of "visuality," or how we see. Filmmakers, designers, and their audiences have enjoyed an explosive period of innovations in the invention, capture, and editing of motion pictures but still struggle to situate themselves vis-à-vis new technologies of representation. The creation and consumption of projected "content" has merged in unexpected ways. The studio delved into the filmic, as much as the architectural, relationship between script and projection, the former usually serving as the template or pretext for filmmaking and the latter manifesting its

increasingly historical mode of delivery and final fruition. Projection precedes script in the studio's equation, with the parameters of the projected image "cast" in roles of formal generation.

Projection—in all of its utopian, geometric, and cinematic dimensions—guided many aspects of the studio, including design methodology and strategy of urban engagement. At a prosaic level, the advent of digital projection has opened the field of screening environments—and, in fact, the typology of the cinema—in unforeseen and largely untested ways. In addition to mapping the basic properties of filmic projection, the students developed and elucidated the relationships between more and less abstract deployments of the concept.

"Scripting" has a brief history in contemporary architecture but an extensive one in filmmaking. In the latter, the script dictates the pace and potential of unfolding drama and establishes the parameters of cinematic effect. The script, or screenplay, describes and narrates scenes that will become filmic environments. Computational scripting for the generation of 2- and 3-D environments is more prescriptive, in the sense that a command will simply be enacted, rather than interpreted by a director, cinematographer, or actor. However, scripts of both kinds elaborate a set of conditions—spatial, emotional, technical, or otherwise.

A number of other terms, innovations, and relationships factored into the studio in important ways: **Projection vs. pixilation**: film, television, video, digital + web-based delivery; **Story structure**: narrative, non-linear, documentary, found footage, reality; **Auteur theory**: Cahier du Cinema, Bazin, Saris, Nouvelle Vague; **Editing methods**: continuous takes, jump-cuts, montage, fade; **Genre**: theatrical, independent, alternative, art film, B-movie, porn, etc.; **Light + sound**: aspect ratios, ambient, brightness, soundtrack.

Overview

The studio began with a few brief, overlapping exercises and research compilations to explore different ways of brokering between the fields of film and architecture, then built toward proposals for a new cinema complex in Los Angeles.

Planar Dissections: Planar dissections are instances in which the same collection of shapes can be combined to create two distinct geometric wholes. Dissections arise out of a film like overlay of tessellation patterns, which we mined for new, "quasi-crystaline" formations.

Film Analysis: Each student selected, edited, and analyzed two sixty-second loops from any source, from a theatrical release to surveillance video, to establish a provisional spectrum of cinematic experience and a personal range of priorities for the semester's work.

(01) Collected NOWplex Studio Work

Precedent Evaluation: Each student was responsible for a thorough architectonic analysis of a historically salient screening venue: a movie palace, multiplex, Kunsthal, installation, and so on.

Exhibitionary Matrix-Manifold: Building on the above research, each student generated a spatial continuum of one million cubic feet of novel screening space. A preliminary study of this continuum was due prior to the studio trip to Los Angeles; a final 1"=20' 3-D print or model was due at the midterm.

Final Project: The studio will culminate in a new center for cinema sited along Los Angeles' Wilshire Boulevard corridor. The NOWplex fills a void in the cultural landscape of L.A. and adds a focal node to the constellation of movie theaters, production studios, film schools, galleries, and museums arrayed across the city.

Program

Los Angeles has pioneered many new architectural and urban paradigms, among them the "enclaves" of movie studios and gated communities as well as the Wilshire corridor's extrusional density, celebrated by Reyner Banham. A more recent, wildly successful but less credited local innovation was what Terence Riley termed the temple-and-barn approach to institutional expansion, inaugurated by Arata Isozaki's and Frank Gehry's MOCA campuses—MoMA and many museums have followed suit. A similar strategy led to the ArcLight, L.A.'s premier multiplex in which a network of fourteen new, state-of-the-art theaters are lodged in a shed behind the existing Cinerama Dome. The NOWplex builds on the logic of barn-and-temple planning without remaining beholden to it. Screening spaces, depending on research and curatorial agenda, take serial or hierarchical forms and occupy half to three-quarters of the overall structure; the remainder houses approximately 100,000 square feet of ancillary,

service, and retail space. The project includes a target of providing parking for three hundred cars.

Site

NOWplex enters a nodal constellation of art and film institutions across greater Los Angeles.

Los Angeles was the most prolific city in the theater-palace building boom, as described by Paul Virilio in *War and Cinema: The Logistics of Perception* (Verso, 1989; originally published in French, 1984), due to two salient local characteristics: Angelenos were building to showcase a local industry, and they were doing so in the first U.S. urban milieu to be scaled more for automobiles than pedestrians.

The site for this studio was on Wilshire Boulevard, where the road turns from the old downtown grid to a true east-west extrusion between MacArthur Park and Koreatown. Our site is at the only remaining high-density stretch of Wilshire, untouched by either L.A.'s long "museum row" or the recent spate of state-of-the-art movie theaters.

Just above Wilshire, two available sites straddle Virgil Street: Site A is kittycorner to the Bollocks Wilshire Building (now housing the Southwestern University Law School), and Site B is a block-to-block open space that sits next to a superior court, the tallest building in the vicinity. Students were instructed to work with either or both sites as well as some intermediate lots for parking.

Appendix: Typological Overview: Advancing Cinema

In contrast to the many movie palaces built throughout the U.S. in the 1920s and 1930s, Constructivist and Bauhaus screening spaces rejected the analogy of cinema to theater: The spaces for viewing film were to be as radically fitted to the potential of the new medium as spaces for opera and Shakespearian drama were once tailored to theirs, not simply a conversion of theatrical venues. The confidence of the European avant-garde in this respect was built on the assumption that filmic art would continue to explore its formal as much as its narrative potential. Opera had clearly subordinated narrative to performative issues of solos, spectacle, and so on, and many early filmmakers and theorists saw film as a logical extension of that trend away from the centrality of storytelling. Whereas traditional movie theaters cast both their performers and their audience into established roles that were reinforced or challenged by the theatrical experience, new architectures of performance, especially for film and music, jettison the dialectic of spectators and players to become spatial "instruments" in the service of a given technology.

The innovations that arose in cinema-specific architecture may be highlighted with three design pairings. In the first pairing, an analogy is drawn between the workings of performance-exhibition space and the relationship between the camera's body and its lens. Walter Gropius' Total Theater (1927) and Frederick Kiesler's Film Guild (1929) both employ "lensing" to redefine viewership through architecture. A "variable theater-instrument," as Gropius put it, the Total Theater operates as if it were a zoom lens to customize the scope and proximity of performance. A rotating "aperture" allows in-the-round, solo, and orchestral staging through a single disc rotation in plan. At the Film Guild, arguably the first cinema dedicated specifically to avant-garde cinema, the main theater is imagined to resemble the internal cavity of a Leica: an immaculate black box is punctuated by a great eye of circular screen, which is bounded by curtaining with various aspect ratios and a spool of white from the projected oculus running up and over the audience.

Two other early cinema buildings explore maximal viewing conditions. In Konstantin Melnikov's Rusakov Club (1928), a three-wing stadium brackets individual and collective assemblies for a 1:5 range in audience size. Though far less revealing of its internal agenda, Riccardo Morandi's Cinematografo Maestoso (1954), in Rome, is possibly the most structurally ambitious screening space ever built—it is almost a hangar-in-the-round, with seven-feet-deep trusses spanning lengthwise, from the screen to the back of the balcony. The pitch of Melnikov's raked seating as it cantilevers out over a Moscow street is echoed in the field of angled skylights that puncture Morandi's roof plane as it descends toward the final window of the screen.

In recent projects by OMA and Coop Himmelb(l)au, the "cinematic" in architecture is understood in complementary terms, either as a black-box space that must be serviced by an externalized architecture or as a pretext for boring through an architectonic solid with an extruded frame for performance. The honeycomb stack of Coop Himmelb(l)au's Dresden multiplex (1998) anchors a far less disciplined system of circulation routes, encased in their own crystalline "projection." OMA's Casa di Musica (2005), by contrast, forces live performance into an essentially cinematic rapport with the cityscape, which is bracketed beyond the proscenium. In both projects, the conventions of film-viewing are less redefined than redeployed against typological presumption: Coop Himmelb(l)au argues against the multiplex, and OMA argues against the theater.

"And they declare it, this drastic medium of the culture industry, popular art . . . "—Theodor Adorno, *Aesthetics and Politics*, (Verso, 2007)

As an exercise, it helps to think of the 1990s shopping mall as fundamentally a cinema multiplex with a load of corollary infrastructure, such as cafés, restaurants, and shops (much as an airport functions today with a new primacy given to what one could call "third-person" retailing). Then think of the coming mall as this same multiplex exploded open so as to allow the infiltration of every unit (indeed every cubic inch) of these locales, not only the shop modules but also the anchor stores, the parking lots, the plaza-ed thoroughfares, the gallerias, the signage. . .

"A new entity has emerged—the 'experience'—and nearly all enterprises have arrived at this, either together or independently."—Sanford Kwinter, *Requiem for the City at the End of the Millennium* (Actar, 2010), p. 46

"These are the five apparent characteristics of the new image: the dispersive situation, the deliberately weak links, the voyage form, the consciousness of clichés, the condemnation of plot. It is the crisis of both the action-image and the American Dream."—Gilles Deleuze, *Cinema 1: Movement-Time* (Les Editions de Minuit, 1983), p. 210

pro·jec·tion (pr-jkshn) n.

1. The act of projecting or the condition of being projected.

2. A thing or part that extends outward beyond a prevailing line or surface: spiky projections on top of a fence; a projection of land along the coast.

3. A plan for an anticipated course of action: "facilities [that] are vital to the projection of U.S. force . . . in the Pacific" (Alan D. Romberg).

4. A prediction or an estimate of something in the future, based on present data or trends.

5. (a) The process of projecting an image onto a screen or other surface for viewing. (b) An image so projected.

6. Mathematics: The image of a geometric figure reproduced on a line, plane, or surface.

7. A system of intersecting lines, such as the grid of a map, on which part or all of the globe or another spherical surface is represented as a plane surface.

8. Psychology: (a) The attribution of one's own attitudes, feelings, or suppositions to others: "Even trained anthropologists have been guilty of unconscious projection of clothing the subjects of their research in theories brought with them into the field" (Alex Shoumatoff). (b) The attribution of one's own attitudes, feelings, or desires to someone or something as a naive or unconscious defense against anxiety or guilt.

pro·jection·al adj.

The American Heritage®
Dictionary of the English Language, fourth edition
2000, Houghton Mifflin Company

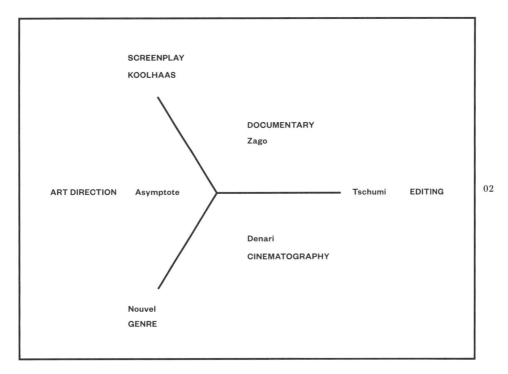

SCREENPLAY
KOOLHAAS

DOCUMENTARY
Zago

ART DIRECTION   Asymptote   Tschumi   EDITING

Denari
CINEMATOGRAPHY

Nouvel
GENRE

(02) Cinema and Architecture Diagram.

"The difference betwccn artists and film-makers is often expressed in terms of the "white cube of the gallery" and the "black box of the theater," respectively. The white cube-black box dyad organizes a number of oppositions between the art and film worlds: the sculptural space of the artists' film opposes the theatrical film's two-dimensionality; the gallery's mobile viewer is distinguished from the seated cinema spectator; the gallery space enables freedom of choice and movement among viewers who come and go on their own time, while the theatrical space of film screenings putatively constricts the viewer's spatial and temporal experience. This last quality of film is often described as a barrier to film's entry into the art world, as it demands a temporal commitment quite different from that of looking at painting or sculpture."—Jonathan Walley, Modes of Film Practice in *The Avant-Garde in Art and the Moving Image (Tate Publishing, Limited, 2008)*, p. 190

"After 1914, while old Europe was being covered with cenotaphs, the Americans, who had suffered fewer losses, were building their great cinema temples—deconsecrated sanctuaries in which, as Paul Morand put it, the public sensed the end of the world in an ambience of profanation and black masses . . . The architectural vocabulary of the American cinema cathedrals was already there in the agglomeration heterogeneous styles, the huge naves and long gangways, the disproportionate central staircase, and above all the imposing technological environment of electricity, lifts, air-conditioning, and so on. Mere commercial logic seemed to go by the board, for the invention of marketing had the result that the whole commodity system of the young industrial civilization henceforth presented itself within immaterial fields of perception." —Paul Virilio, *War and Cinema*, Verso, p. 31

Bibliography

Cinema + Architecture

Tschumi, Bernard. *The Manhattan Transcripts*. Cambridge: The MIT Press, 1994.

Foster, Hal. *The Art-Architecture Complex*. London: Verso, 2011.

Penz, François, and Maureen Thomas, eds. *Cinema & Architecture: Melies, Mallet-Stevens, Multimedia*. London: British Film Institute, 1997.

Virilio, Paul. *War and Cinema: The Logistics of Perception*. London: Verso, 1989.

Zizek, Slavoj. *Organs without Bodies: On Deleuze and Consequences*. Abingdon: Routledge, 2004.

Grainge, Paul, Mark Jancovich, and Sharon Monteith, eds. *Film Histories: An Introduction and Reader*. Toronto: University of Toronto Press, 2007.

Shiel, Mark, and Tony Fitzmaurice, eds. *Cinema and the City: Film and Urban Societies in a Global Context*. Oxford: Blackwell Publishers, 2001.

Lamster, Mark, ed. *Architecture and Film*. New York: Princeton Architectural Press, 2000.

Film/Video/New Media

Young, Paul. *Art Cinema*. Edited by Paul Duncan. London: Taschen, 2009.

Lavin, Sylvia. *Kissing Architecture*. Princeton: Princeton University Press, 2011.

Aitken, Doug. *Broken Screen: Expanding the Image, Breaking the Narrative*. New York: D.A.P./Distributed Art Publishers, 2006.

Deleuze, Gilles. *Cinema 1: The Movement-Image*. Minneapolis: The University of Minnesota Press, 1987.

Deleuze, Gilles. *Cinema 2: The Time-Image*. Minneapolis: The University of Minnesota Press, 1989.

Leighton, Tanya, ed. *Art and the Moving Image: A Critical Reader*. London: Tate Publishing, 2008.

Martin, Sylvia, ed. *Video Art*. London: Taschen, 2006.

Cornell, Lauren, Massimiliano Gioni, and Laura Hoptman. *Younger than Jesus: The Reader*. Göttingen: Steidl & Partners, 2009.

Jay, Martin. "Scopic Regimes of Modernity." In *Vision and Visuality*, edited by Hal Foster. New York: The New Press, 1998.

LA/Wilshire

Banham, Reyner. *Los Angeles: The Architecture of Four Ecologies*. Berkeley, University of California Press, 2009.

Rodrick, Kevin. *Wilshire Boulevard: Grand Concourse*. Santa Monica: Angel City Press, 2005.

Varnelis, Kazys, ed. *The Infrastructural City: Networked Ecologies in Los Angeles*. New York: Actar, 2009.

Southern, John. *Wilshire Star Maps: An Abbreviated Guide*. Los Angeles: Urban Operations, 2011.

Stenger, Josh. "Return to Oz: The Hollywood Redevelopment Project, or Film History as Urban Renewal." In *Film Histories: An Introduction and Reader*, edited by Paul Grainge, Mark Jancovich, and Sharon Monteith. Toronto: University of Toronto Press, 2007.

Maltzan, Michael. *No More Play: Conversations on Urban Speculation in Los Angeles and Beyond*. Edited by Jessica Varner. Ostfildern: Hatje Cantz, 2011.

Zaero-Polo, Alejandro. "The Politics of the Envelope, Part I." *Log* 13/14 (2008).

Zaero-Polo, Alejandro. "The Politics of the Envelope, Part II." *Log* 16 (2009).

Kwinter, Sanford. *Requiem for the City at the End of the Millennium*, New York: Actar, 2010.

NOWplex: A Center for Contemporary Cinema

1-Movies, though, are often the better gamble: Avatar's $3.5 billion in revenue-to-date, after a cost of $350 million, will soon eclipse the $4.1 billion price tag of the Burj Kalifa, most of that likely to never be recouped.

2-This irony can be seen in a more positive light: Though the product of theater owners' terror at the rise of home theaters, post-THX and IMAX cineplexes are a rare and welcome instance of new public space born of commercial desperation. On the other hand, art in projection has become a prime means of interrogating space, whether the pristine volumes of the gallery or the found possibilities of adaptive reuse. Cf. Sylvia Lavin, *Kissing Architecture* (Princeton Architectural Press, 2011) and Hal Foster, *The Art-Architecture Complex* (Verso, 2011).

Studio Work

Filmic: Auteur-Architect Convergence (or Time and Space Sequencing)

The media of film and architecture are the most widely experienced forms of cultural production today. While the roles of the auteur and architect were at one point analogous within their respective disciplines, developments within the past twenty years in the production of film and architecture have rendered the role of the single author virtually obsolete. With the emergence of building-information-modeling software and the ongoing distribution or specialization of project oversight, the auteur, in both the filmic and architectural sense, has forgone artistic control in favor of market-driven modes of production.

The following projects have reengaged the role of the auteur as architect, carefully analyzing the structure of film as a way to challenge preconceived traditions of storytelling and space-making. The convergence of the auteur-architect produces three schemes that challenge the cinema building type through non-linear spatial sequencing and material layering, blurring the distinction between the real, the imagined, and the projected image.

Amir Mikhaeil—Time-Image

"This is what happens when the image becomes time-image...the screen itself is the cerebral membrane where immediate and direct confrontations take place between the past and the future, the inside and the outside, at a distance impossible to determine, independent of any fixed point. The image no longer has space and movement as its primary characteristics but topology and time."—Gilles Deleuze, *Cinema 2: The Time-Image*

Neither a multiplex nor a museum, the new Center for Contemporary Cinema, situated near the periphery of downtown L.A., along Wilshire Boulevard, implants a new manifold for the projection of film and new media in the city. By collapsing multiple planes of image, both filmic and real, the project seeks to bridge the turn along Wilshire from its true east-west axis toward the downtown grid. Taking cues from Tarkovsky's representation of time in cinema and the Deleuzian conception of the "time-image," which is not reliant on the linear progression of movement through film, the project seeks to "jump" the turn, dislocating the continuous urban narrative structure of Wilshire Boulevard. Located on the corner of Wilshire Boulevard and Virgil Avenue, the massing of the building turns as it rises to realign itself toward downtown.

The turn creates an internal cascading atrium straddled by two primary hyperbolic surfaces. Two primary theater blocks attach themselves to either side of the atrium. The smaller block contains a single theater facing inward, toward the lobby level, while the larger block contains four theaters and culminates at the top with the largest theater, which faces the city through a proscenium. Both the audience and projected film are visible through this proscenium to gallery attendees and viewers within the atrium. From the street, the multiple figures, lights, shadows, and images collapsing onto one another are visible as a flickering image that announces the cinema center's presence and activities.

The proliferation of simultaneous activities and the superposition of images and figures within the cinema center reflect in built form the transition from the movement-image of classical cinema to the time-image. In *Cinema 2: The Time- Image*, Gilles Deleuze describes this transition as a reversal of the subordination of time to movement, where "time ceases to be the measurement of normal."

01

(01) Massing model shown in the context of Wilshire Boulevard

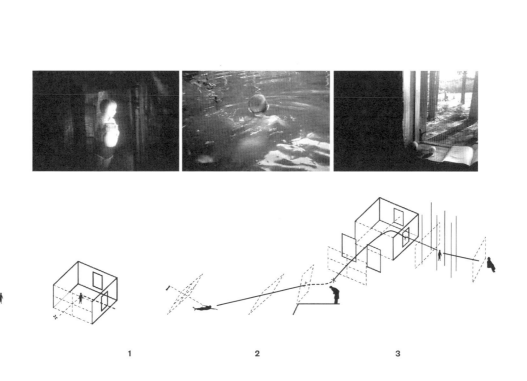

1   2   3

Scene 12: One Body So Solitary

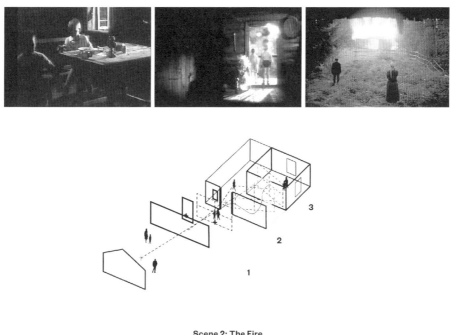

3

2

1

Scene 2: The Fire

(02) Early filmic analysis of Tarkovsky's *Mirror*. Diagrams map the
non-linear progression of movement through two scenes in the film.

03

Amir Mikhaeil—Time-Image

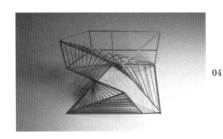

04

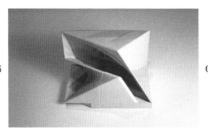

05

06

(03) Model view, showing the north circulation system. (04) Study model of building geometry, showing the twisting of the building mass. The turn in the building aligns the mass toward downtown Los Angeles. (05) Section model shown closed. The internal hyperbolic surfaces can be seen above the cascading atrium. (06) Section model shown open.

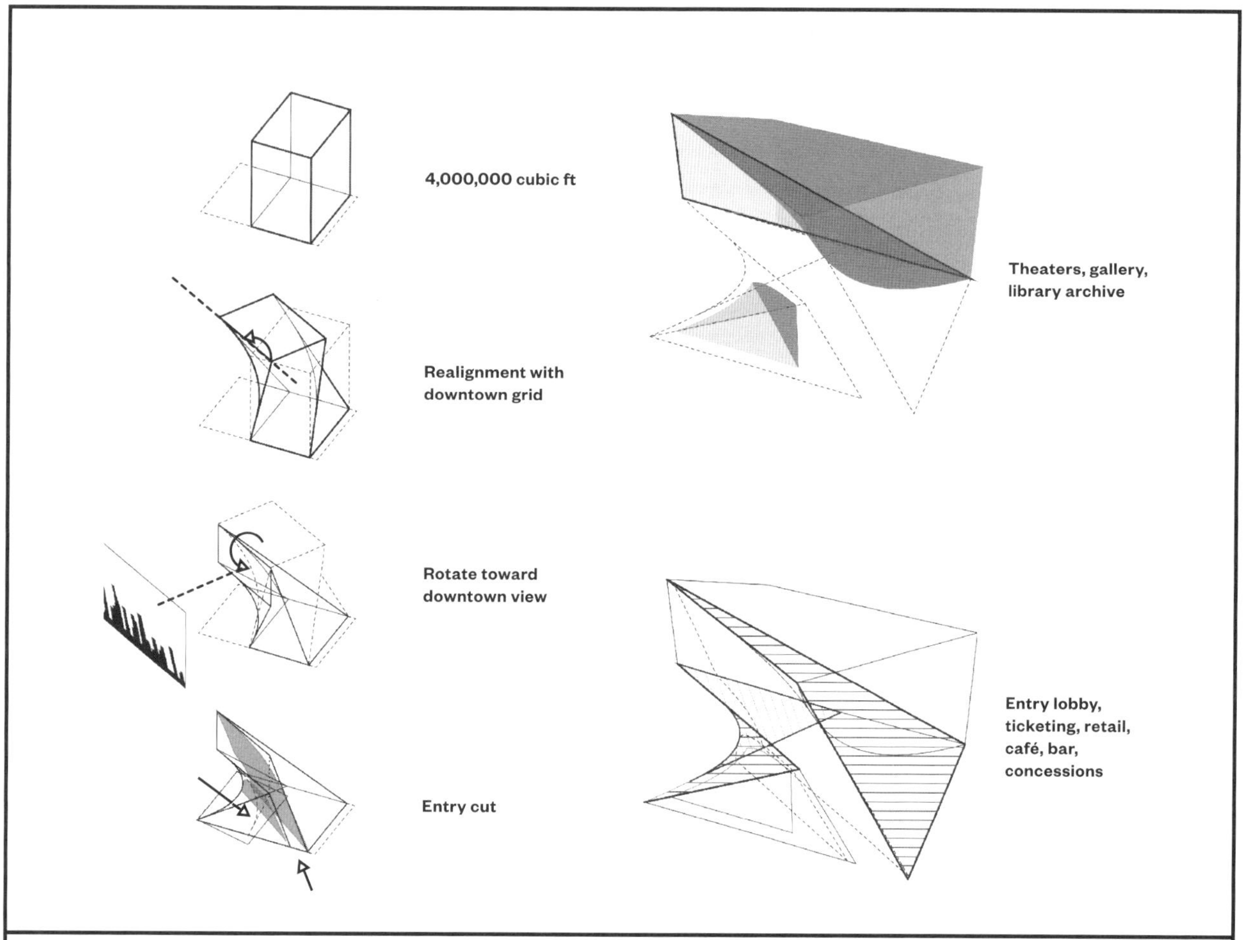

4,000,000 cubic ft

Realignment with downtown grid

Rotate toward downtown view

Entry cut

Theaters, gallery, library archive

Entry lobby, ticketing, retail, café, bar, concessions

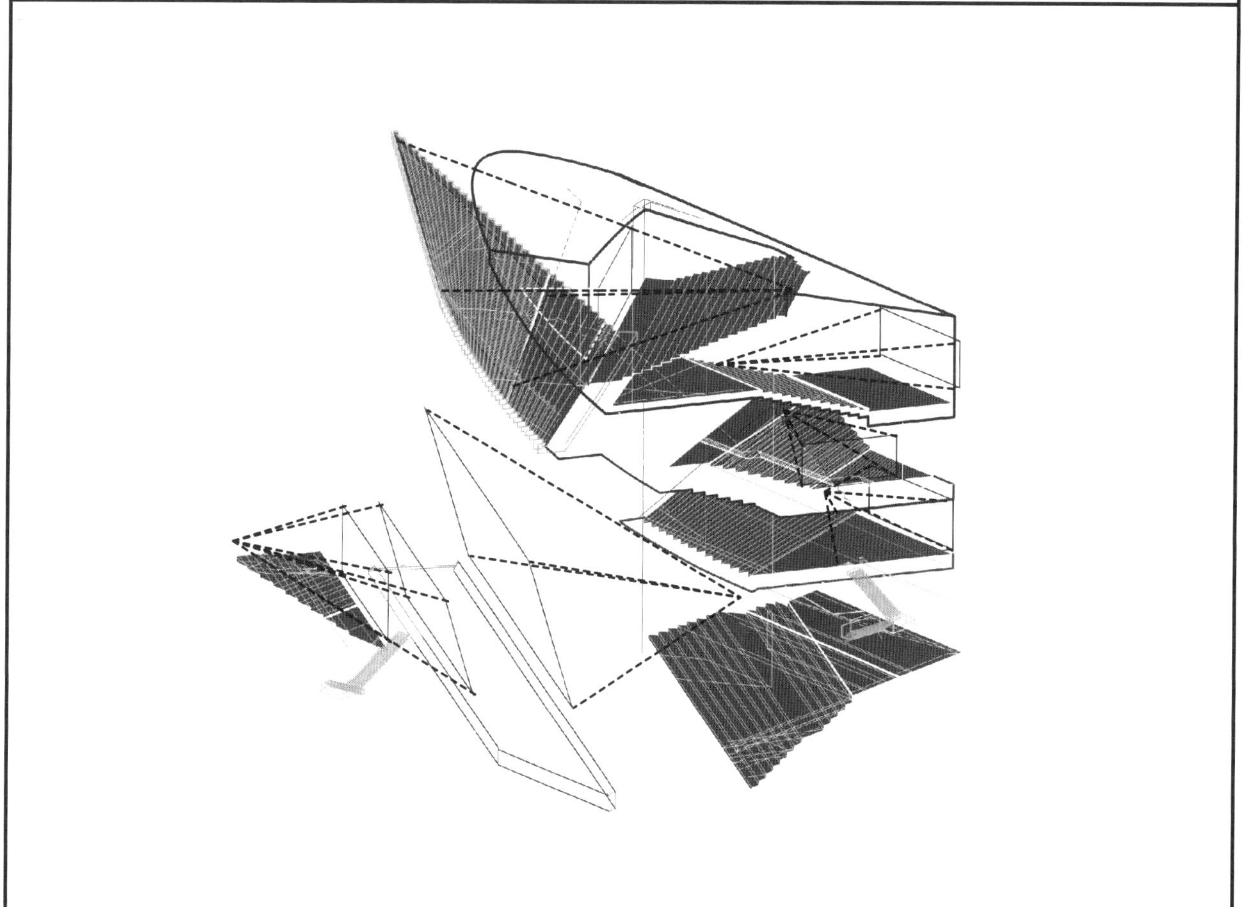

(07) Massing and program diagrams. The massing is driven by the twisting action of orienting the proposal toward the center of Los Angeles. Theater, library, and archive program occupies the volumes on either side of the entry cut. (08) Axonometric diagram, showing the stacking of theaters.

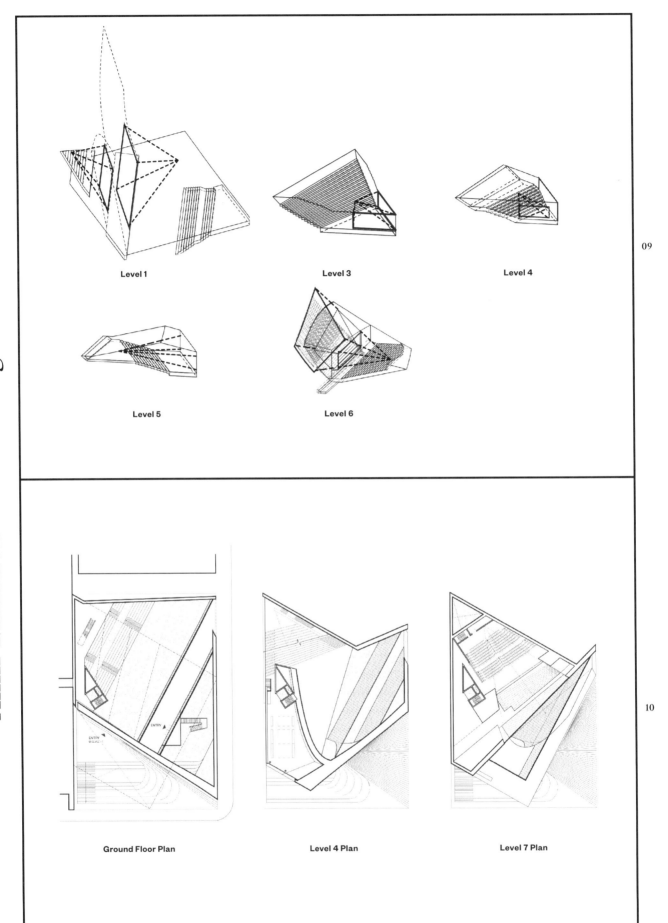

Amir Mikhaeil—Time-Image

Level 1

Level 3

Level 4

Level 5

Level 6

09

Ground Floor Plan

Level 4 Plan

Level 7 Plan

10

(09) Catalog diagram of the multiple theaters in the proposal. (10)
Floor plans. The entry leads to the large, cascading atrium, which
rises through the building adjacent to the theater volumes above.

NOW _ PLEX

(11) Rendering of the building entry on Wilshire Boulevard,
showing steps lead down from street level to the entrance. (12) View
of the upper-theater-level promenade, showing the largest screen.

01—Joe Day, NOWplex —The Studio Work—pp. 32–33

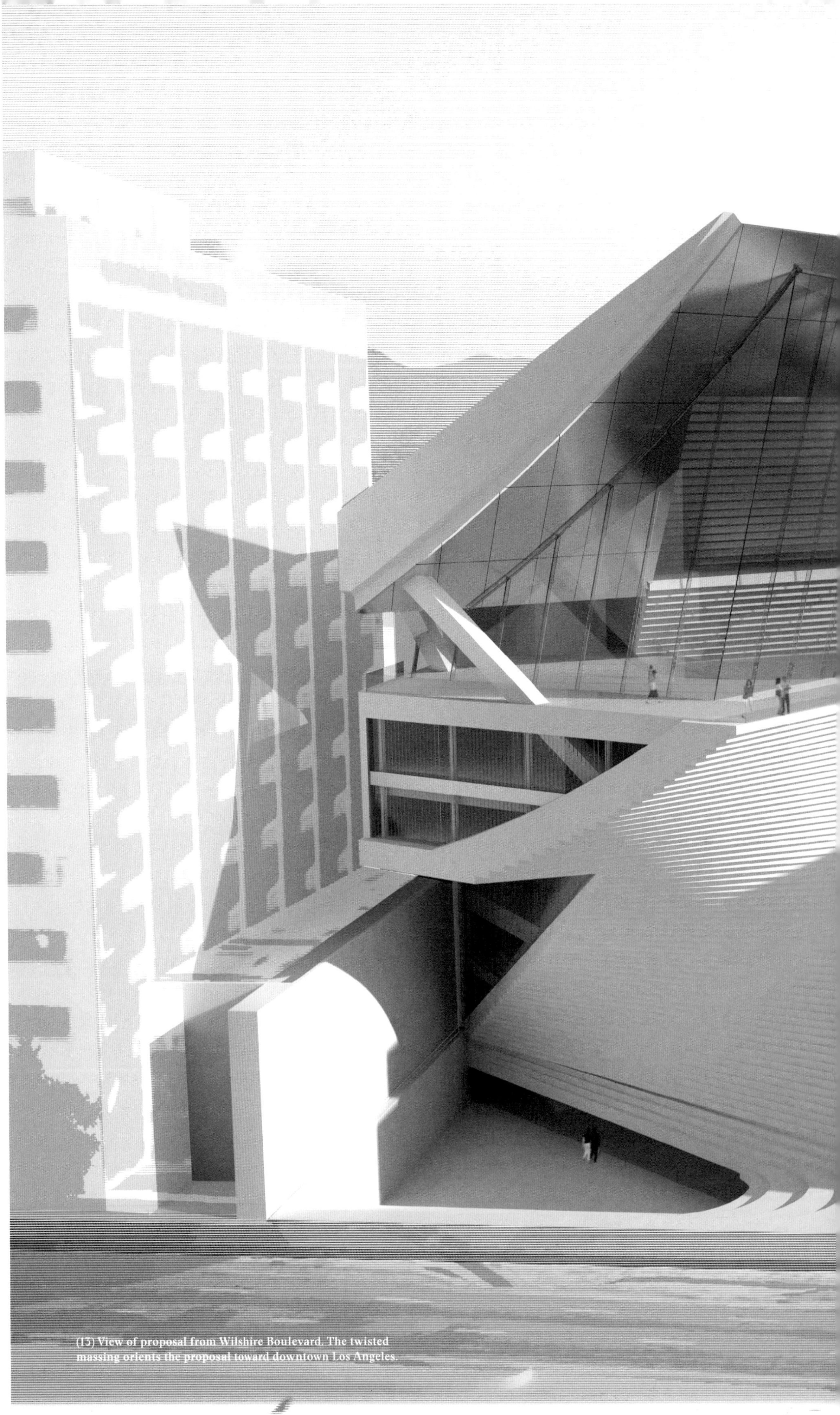

Amir Mikhaeil—Time-Image

(15) View of proposal from Wilshire Boulevard. The twisted massing orients the proposal toward downtown Los Angeles.

15

Lauren Chapman—Déjà Vu

This project began with an analysis of the film *Vertigo*. A close reading of the movie illuminated Hitchcock's use of interwoven technical strategies to create multi-dimensional cinematic space. Analysis uncovered an intricate, self-referential structure that, much like the narrative, operates as an abstract puzzle one can detect but would be hard-pressed to solve. The proposed cinema aims to create space, both concrete and abstract, using a similar strategy.

Beginning with a set of simple constraints—a cubic grid, three-point surfaces, and central axis of rotation—spatial orders were defined and then mutated through a series of formal manipulations. The result is a faintly symmetrical cube with four unique facades and spiraling circulation weaving between a central atrium and ribbon views of Wilshire Boulevard. Each floor, or horizontal cut, provides a new reference by which to measure spatial transformation from the previous floor. Full-height interior views from the atrium balcony allow the subject to absorb the visual clues provided by the vertical cross section, while tighter interior spaces refocus the subject on the immediate spatial and programmatic experience.

01

02

(01/02) Stills from the restaurant scene in Alfred Hitchcock's *Vertigo* show the multidimensional space created through technical strategies.

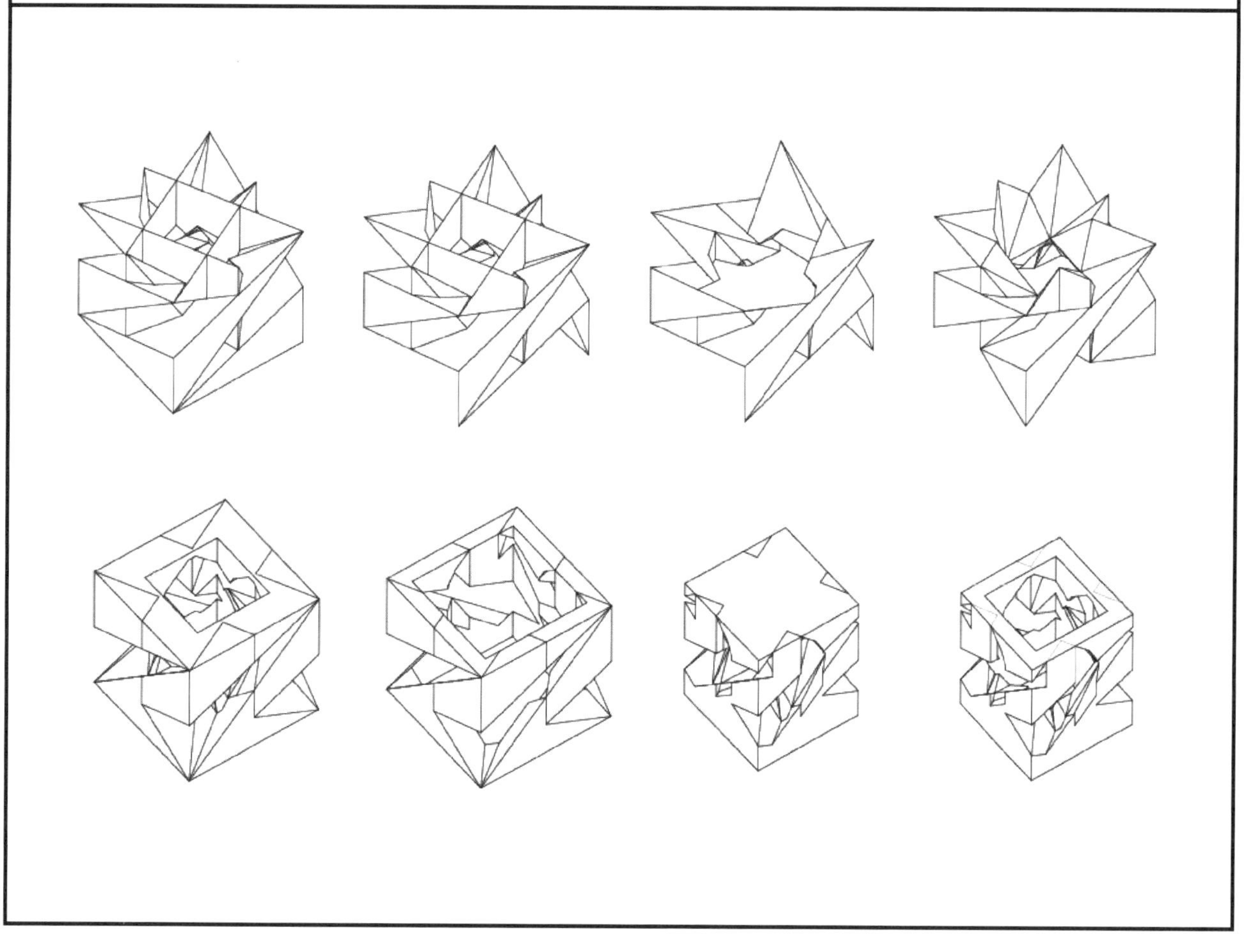

(03) This spatial analysis of the restaurant scene from *Vertigo* shows Alfred Hitchcock's use of filming techniques to create multidimensional space. (04) Using the strategies of multidimensional-volume creation learned through the filmic analysis, these early formal diagrams show alternative approaches to the proposal's overall massing.

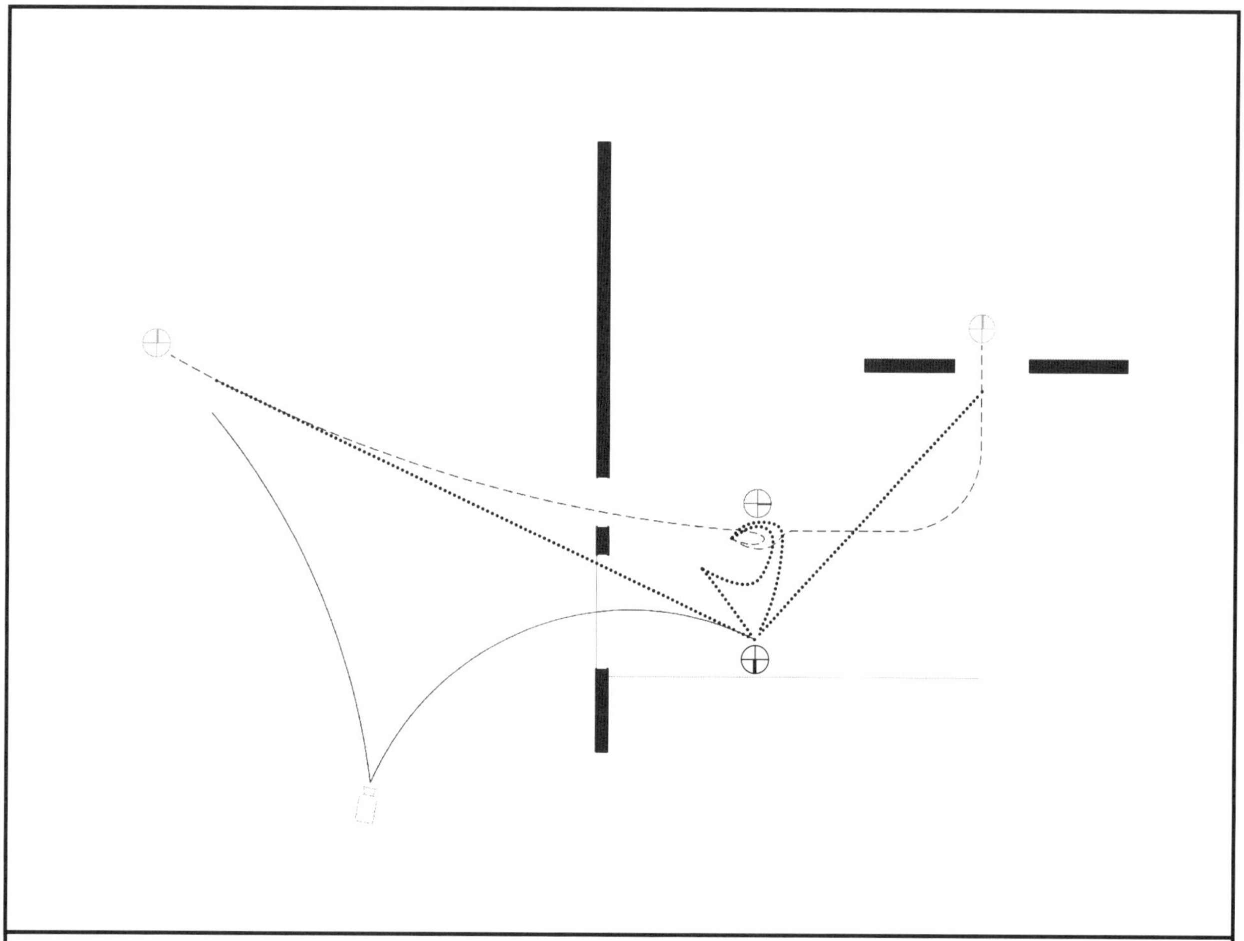

Lauren Chapman—Déjà Vu

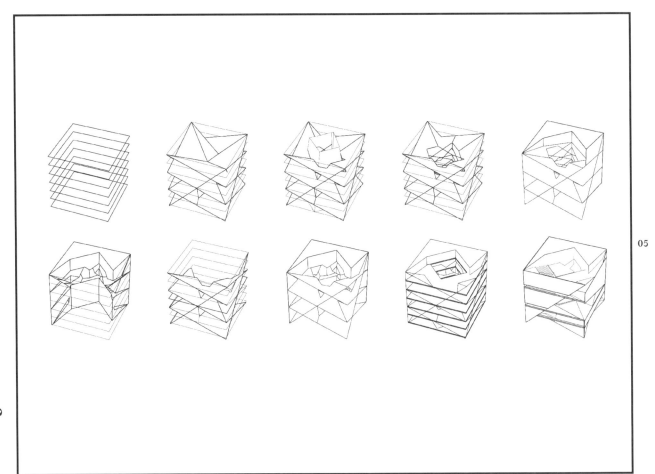

05

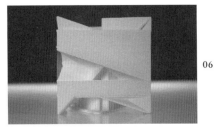

06

07

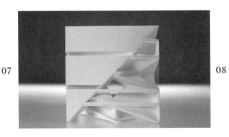

08

(05) This design process diagram shows the transformation of cubic geometry using three-point surfaces to arrive at the final proposal arrangement. (06/07/08) Final model, north/east/south/west elevations.

09

10

(09) View along Wilshire Boulevard, showing the primary facade. The spiraling interior circulation pattern and varied three-point surfaces are visible on the interior. (10) Interior view, showing the central atrium. The varied surfaces reflect the transformation of space from floor to floor. Views out toward Wilshire and Virgil are provided through ribbon windows and larger, transparent zones on the facades.

Ilsa Falis—In the Mood

This project calls for the creation of a center for contemporary cinema on a site off Wilshire Boulevard in downtown Los Angeles. Based on initial analyses of film and how it is viewed, the design creates different types of spaces in which an audience member can have calibrated interactions with media.

This aim is achieved by the projection of traditional theaters from a spiraling circulation core that stretches between two shed like masses. These masses relate to the street via large glazed facades that double as projection surfaces for traditional theater seating. This configuration creates an urban spectacle as well as an experience that allows for multiple projections to be viewed simultaneously. In addition, the winding circulation path that provides access to these theaters is defined by a system of louvers that allow sound and light to leak into the public areas of the building. This provides visitors the opportunity to move freely through a variety of film-viewing environments, thereby taking an active role in a self-curated experience of film and projected media.

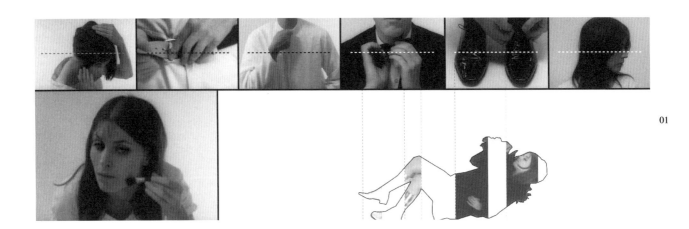

(01) Film analysis diagram of Kar Wai Wong's *In the Mood for Love*, highlighting the director's inclusion of the viewer in the scene through the use of camera angles and cropped shots.

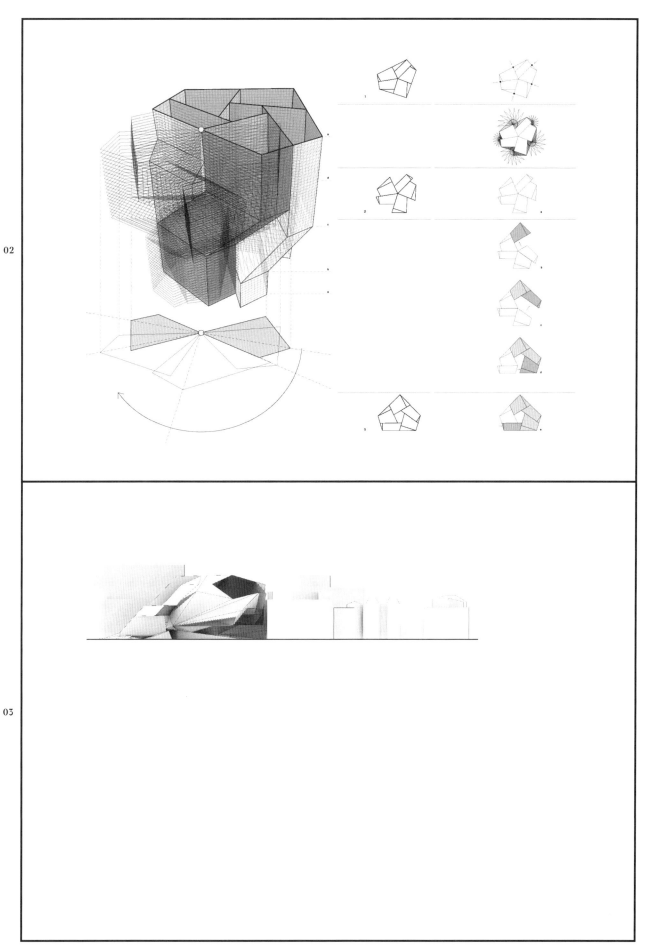

03

(02) Planar dissection diagram, showing the transformation of two-dimensional geometry into a different pattern through three-dimensional manipulation. (03) Elevations from Virgil Avenue.

Ilsa Falis—In the Mood

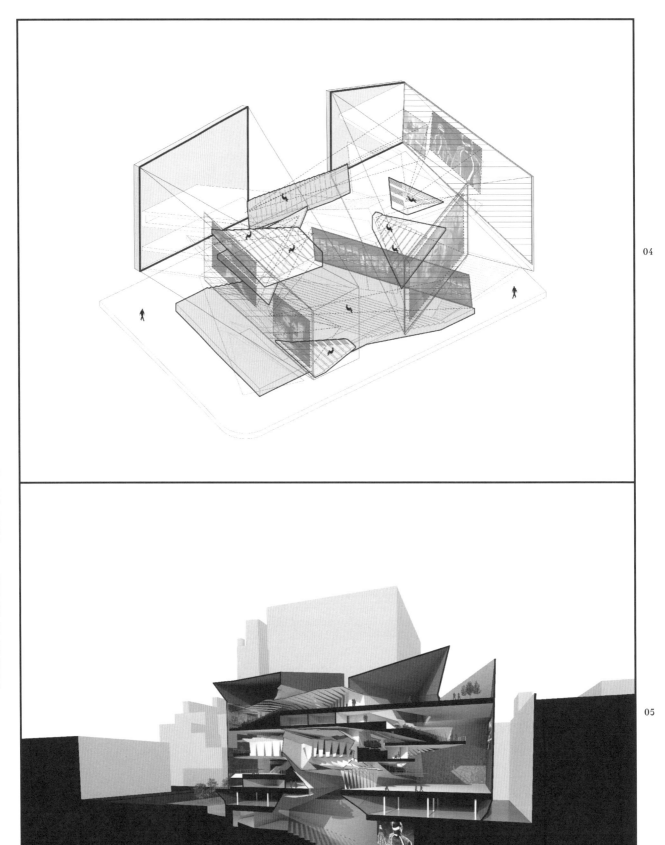

(04) Axonometric diagram, showing screening spaces and projection
surfaces. (05) Rendered building section, highlighting circulation path
and louvered, fractured "skin" stretching between "shed" masses.

(06) Rendered view, showing stacked projecting theaters within the
Virgil Avenue "shed." (07) Rendered view, showing theater space within
the circulation bridge. (08) Rendered view, showing louvered circula
tion bridge.

09

10

(09) Rendered view, showing building's context on Wilshire Boulevard and highlighting the "urban screen." (10) Aerial rendering, showing building's massing and context along the Wilshire Boulevard corridor.

Typological: The Cinema House and the City

The following projects provide new architecture for a contemporary cinematic experience and for an increasingly "filmic" urban condition. In all three schemes, the building typology of the cinema house within the context of Los Angeles is reconceptualized either at the scale of the city as a distributed urban intervention or at the scale of an architectural element or sign. Each strategy examines the claiming of urban space through branding devices, new spatial orders, and structural sequencing spawned by new media. Project and projection mapping was a distinct driver, as each student explored both geometrically and spatially confined conical projection.

Danielle Duryea—Marquee Theater

This new center for cinema is sited along the Wilshire corridor in Los Angeles. The project began with a study of traditional Los Angeles cinema houses and their presence within the city fabric. The main intent for this project was to heighten the experience of leaving the city and entering the world of cinema. In each cinema house studied, the marquee acts as a threshold, which marks the territory where one leaves the city and enters the spectacle of cinema. The marquee has multiple functions: it is an icon for theater, it signifies the program from an urban context, and it often takes on a three-dimensional quality, creating an exterior covered space that forms the transition from the street to lobby.

This project takes the formal language of the traditional marquee and creates a contemporary, inhabitable icon in the form of a centralized tower. While the marquee traditionally is recognized as an additive element projecting information to the city, this scheme pulls the tower to the back of the site, drawing visitors into the center of the project before they circulate outward, to the theater volumes. The marquee tower itself is a series of stacked vertical projection spaces available to new media artists, while the surrounding buildings house normative black-box theaters.

The central marquee brings together the world of commercialized cinema and experimental projection art into a single institution. While the root of the term marquee means "edge" or "border," the proposed marquee tower defines the center of the project, inverting the cinema's dichotomous relationship between inside and outside. As a variation on the traditional single-volume typology of the cinema, this project aims to draw the public into the heart of new media culture, increasing public accessibility by turning the building inside out.

01

(01) Los Angeles cinema houses and their marquees provide the formal ambition for the project.

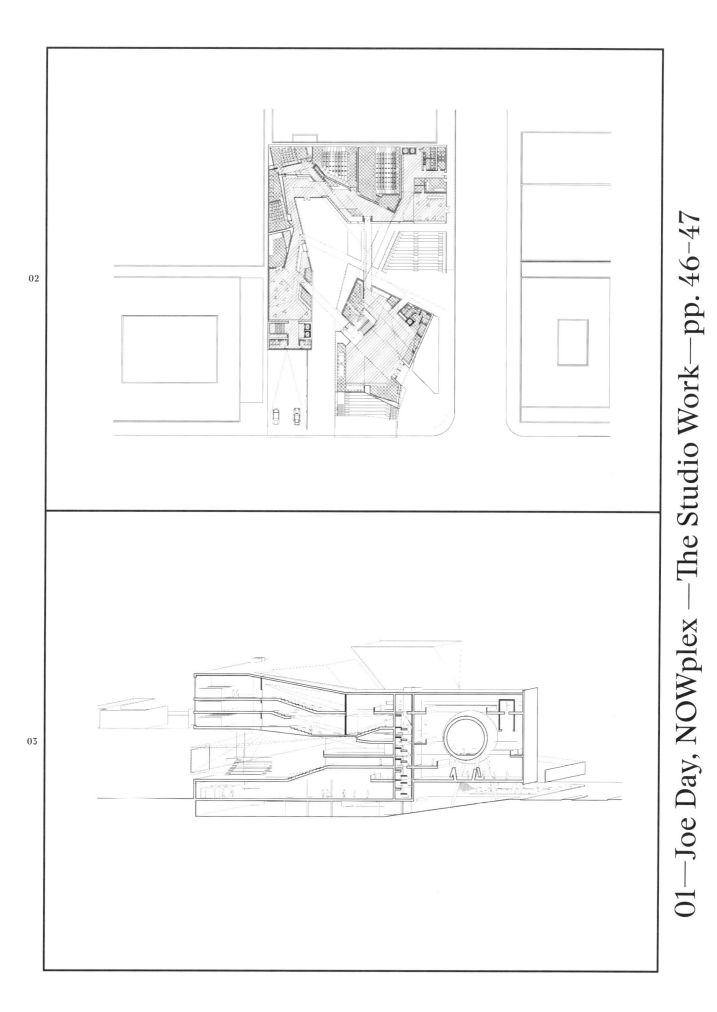

02

03

(02) Ground-level plan, showing the centralized marquee
tower and its surrounding theaters. (03) Sectional axonometric
drawing, cutting through the western edge of the project. The
immersive projection space can be seen to the right, along with
the film archive and smaller theaters.

04

Danielle Duryea—Marquee Theater

05

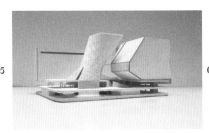

06

07

(04) Progress model, showing view from Virgil Avenue and looking
toward the central marquee tower. (05) Aerial view of the final model.
The marquee tower is flanked by the theater spaces at the edges of
the site. (06) Final model, showing street-level perspective. (07) Final
model, showing aerial view and the project context.

(08) View from the corner of Wilshire Boulevard and Virgil Avenue, looking toward the marquee tower. (09) View from the back outdoor theater, looking toward the marquee tower.

Michael Holborn—Transsaccadic Distortions

This project aims to develop a spatial sequence that will alter the occupant's sense of time and velocity. In order to find ways to disrupt a linear progression of spaces, early analyses tested various scalar relationships and room adjacencies that could challenge the cinema's traditional typological layout. Formally, the geometry of the project is articulated through the idea of movement, with the torqued building mass conceptually reflecting the speed of Wilshire Boulevard.

The faceted wrapping of the exterior envelope further draws upon the geometry of the projection cones themselves, a device that directs an image across space and transports the viewer to another place and time. Theater volumes are broken down and distributed around the periphery of the building volume, allowing visitors to visually engage with viewing

rooms from a spiral circulation system. The visitor's path through the building culminates atop the parking structure, which houses a drive-in theater, expanding the immediate site context of the cinema outward, toward the city. Both the pedestrian path and the car route engage with the cinema at different levels. These forms of moving traffic silmultaneously activate both the ground and the roof plane of the cinema.

Centripetal in organization, the theater's projection surfaces line the exterior envelope, allowing for images to illuminate the Wilshire skyline by projecting an array of graphic imagery from within. By combining a spiral circulation system and a redistributed spatial organization, the multiplex serves as an expression of motion media and the speed of Los Angeles itself.

01

(01) The diagram studies the perspective of the protagonists (Ayrton Senna in the race car and Thomas in profile) and the mechanisms through which these perspectives are created.

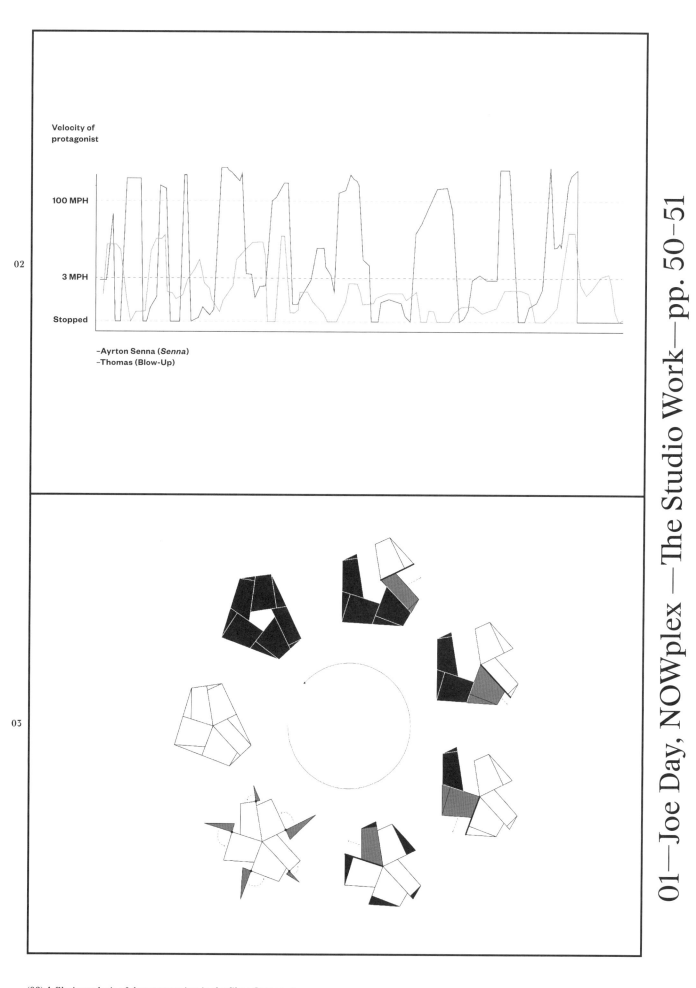

Velocity of
protagonist

100 MPH

3 MPH

Stopped

–Ayrton Senna (*Senna*)
–Thomas (Blow-Up)

02

03

(02) A filmic analysis of the protagonists in the films *Senna* and
Blow-Up. The diagram charts the velocity of the protagonist
throughout the film. (03) The diagram above shows the step-by-step
process of sliding and rotating of the pieces of the overall polygon.
Through these moves, the shape remains the same, but the overall
area of the polygon is increased.

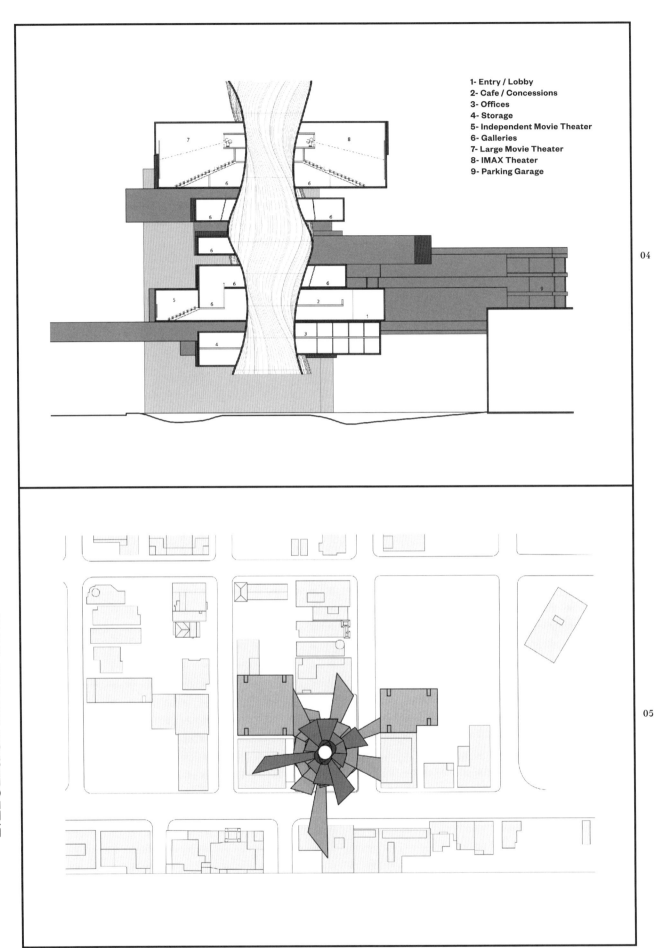

1- Entry / Lobby
2- Cafe / Concessions
3- Offices
4- Storage
5- Independent Movie Theater
6- Galleries
7- Large Movie Theater
8- IMAX Theater
9- Parking Garage

Michael Holborn—Transsaccadic Distortions

04

05

(04) Progress building section, showing the organization of the
building program around a central core space. (05) Progress site plan,
showing the relationship of the building to the surrounding context.

06

07  08  09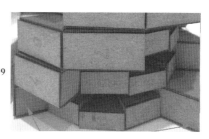

(06) Massing study, showing the process by which the organization
of the theater spaces was created. (07/08/09) Progress model shown
in the larger context model.

Michael Holborn—Transsaccadic Distortions

(10) Interior rendering, showing theater space in which the film is projected onto an adjacent building. This gesture dismantles the preconceived spatial understanding of the projected surface. (11) An aerial night rendering showing how projections reach out to the surrounding context to extend the program beyond the limits of the building envelope. (12) Final building section showing the organization of the building program around a central core space.

Will Fox—Wilshire Cinema Corridor

Los Angeles, like many American cities, suffers from high office vacancy rates in its urban center. With a vacancy rate twice that of New York City's and Chicago's, Los Angeles has the potential to repurpose this unused space as cultural capital. As more free standing cinema houses and theater corporations undergo economic hardship, the opportunity arises to reclaim vacant commercial space for the projection and consumption of cinema.

Alongside urban research, filmic analyses of P. T. Anderson's *Punch Drunk Love* and Jean-Luc Godard's *Contempt* were undertaken to dissect two unique time-and-space sequences. While Anderson captured space as a continuous tracking shot, which absorbs the viewer into the scene's elapsed present, Godard's presents fragments of time in the form of jump-cuts, which conflate past and present. The relationship between continuity (the repetition of consistent frames) and disjunction (the repetition of jump-cuts) animates the possibility of a new cinema typology.

The proposed design for a single cineplex is broken down and surgically redistributed along the length of Wilshire Boulevard. The cinema program is designed to reuse the structural and circulatory core of existing office buildings while allowing for commercial activities to remain uninterrupted. Screening spaces are pushed to the exterior face of the existing buildings, creating a new experience for pedestrian and vehicular viewers alike. The scheme poses an alternative to the singular, freestanding movie palaces of Los Angeles by proposing a series of cinematic installments within the existing city, collectively forming a cinema corridor along Wilshire Boulevard.

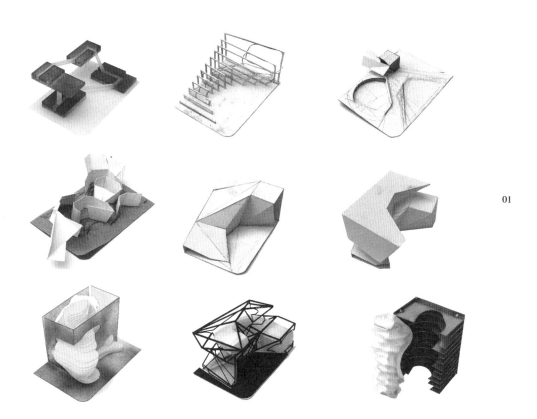

01

(01) Study models, used to explore program adjacencies and projection concepts.

Will Fox—Wilshire Cinema Corridor

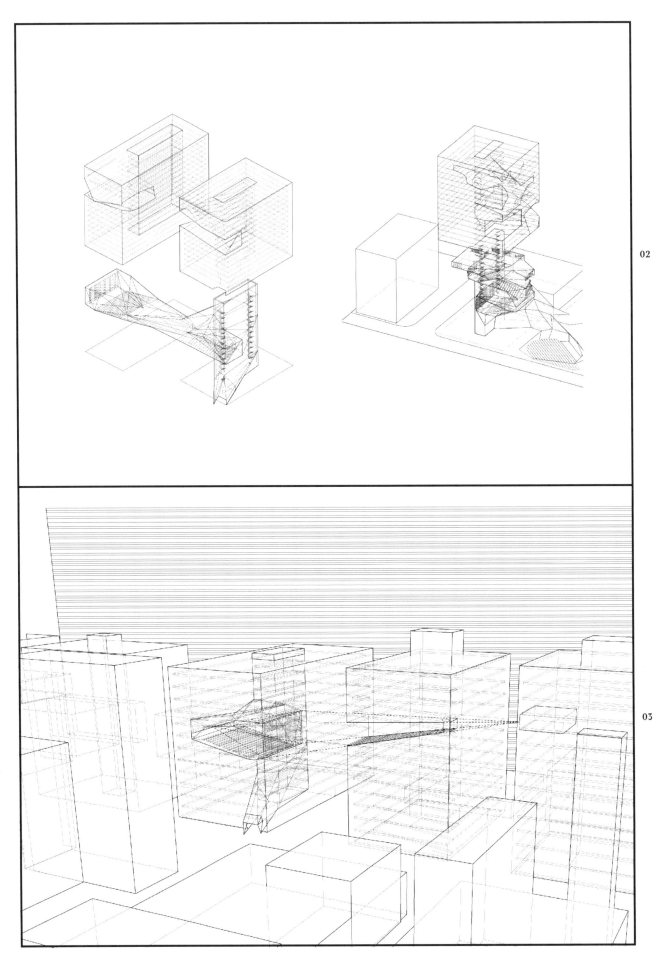

02

03

(02) Diagram of the repurposed vertical circulation of the new
theater, situated in an existing office space at 3440 Wilshire Boulevard
and main cinema hub, situated in an existing office at 3050 Wilshire
Boulevard. (03) This diagram shows the concept for public amphithe-
aters, which are created by separating the projector, seating, and screen
across the upper floors of three buildings.

04

05

06

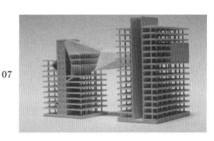

07

08

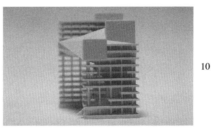

09

10

(04) A large sectional model of the proposal for 3050 Wilshire Boulevard, showing the detailed organization of the lobby and screening rooms adjacent to typical office program. (05/06/07/08/09) Model of 3050 Wilshire Boulevard proposal. (10) Model for 3050 Wilshire Boulevard, showing the main entrance shaped by an exterior amphitheater.

Will Fox—Wilshire Cinema Corridor

(11) View from Wilshire Boulevard of the theater proposal for 3342 Wilshire. The theater program occupies vacant office space and is expressed on the exterior. (12) View from Wilshire Boulevard of the theater proposal for 3440 Wilshire. The theater program occupies vacant office space and is expressed on the exterior.

Technological: Scripting and Projection

The script, or the screenplay, of a film describes and narrates the scenes that will become filmic environments. It dictates the pace and structure of unfolding drama, establishing the parameters of cinematic effect. In contemporary architecture, computational scripting has a brief history and a wide range of application and interpretation. While a "command" will simply be enacted rather than interpreted by a director, cinematographer, or actor, a designer is responsible for the interpretation and the use of the resulting product. In this sense, the architect not only uses technology as a tool but also as a methodology to conceptualize and translate the possibilities of its outcome.

Christos Bolos—Wilshire Theater

The Wilshire Theater investigates the state of contemporary film and its architectural implications in terms of commercial cinematography, new-media art, and emerging technology. In 2011, all the remaining manufacturers of motion-picture cameras ceased production, opting to concentrate entirely on their digital products and essentially freezing the stock of motion-picture films. Meanwhile, all commercial theaters completed the transition to entirely digital projection equipment. Furthermore, advances in high-definition LCD technology have made possible screen sizes comparable to those in feature-film cinemas. This technology now demands our attention as a logical replacement for the obsolete projection techniques of displaying motion pictures. This project, a center for contemporary cinema, attempts to synthesize these issues in an architectural response indicative of this unique moment in media.

Filmic and geometric analyses were pursued as a means to develop an architectural strategy for the theater. For this proposal, the films *Apollo 18, The Blair Witch Project*, and *The Killing Room* were studied for their commonality as found-footage films—productions that attempt to deceive their audience into perceiving them as nonfiction by appearing to be an amateur recording or surveillance footage. Each film was either produced or set in a different time period, using or emulating the recording technology of its time. The analysis for this project thus centered on the apparatuses either used or mimicked in these films. The film stock used was recorded and all scene transitions were indexed to catalog the number of separate cameras used for each film. This information helped to determine the exact type of camera and film stock each scene used, the specifications of each, and the formats in which the films were ultimately disseminated.

The formal diagram for the building was derived from a heptagon composed of shapes that can recombine to form two, smaller heptagons. The transformation between these two states was extrapolated and cataloged, and key frames of the transformation were overlaid into a composite drawing to create a heterogeneous composition while avoiding a singular, fixed geometry. Reinterpreted as an axonometric view, this composite was given volume using localized symmetry to create a final three-dimensional diagram for the theater.

This project addresses the need for dedicated venues for film projection and proposes an architectural response to emerging LCD technologies. At its base, the Wilshire Theater houses screening spaces for all widespread, traditional formats. Each theater and screen is proportionally sized to provide an optimal picture quality for 70-millimeter film. The uppermost volume of the theater contains the LCD—that is, digital—display spaces, immersive video-art exhibition space, and a large-format theater for screening feature films. These screening spaces use high-definition and uniformly backlit, dynamic LCD displays to provide a sharp cinema-quality picture while allowing for transparency and interaction of space. Furthermore, these areas take advantage of digital display technology and its capacity to allow ambient light to enter screening volumes, consequently transforming traditional cinema interiors.

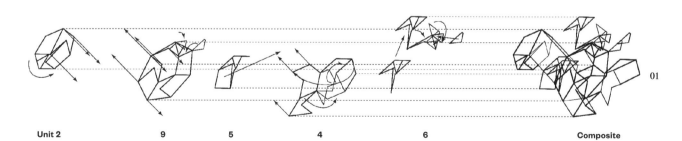

Unit 2   9   5   4   6   Composite

01

(01) Geometric composite axonometric diagram, showing the overlay of various key frames in the manipulation of the heptagon. The resulting composite is given volume to inform the massing of the proposal.

1- APOLLO 18 (1974)

	Instance 01	Instance 02	Instance 03	Instance 04
Camera 01				
Camera 02				
Camera 03				
Camera 04				
Camera 05				
Camera 06				

2- THE BLAIR WITCH PROJECT (1994)

	Instance 01	Instance 02
Camera 01		
Camera 02		

3- THE KILLING ROOM (2008)

	Instance 01	Instance 02
Camera 01		
Camera 02		
Camera 03		

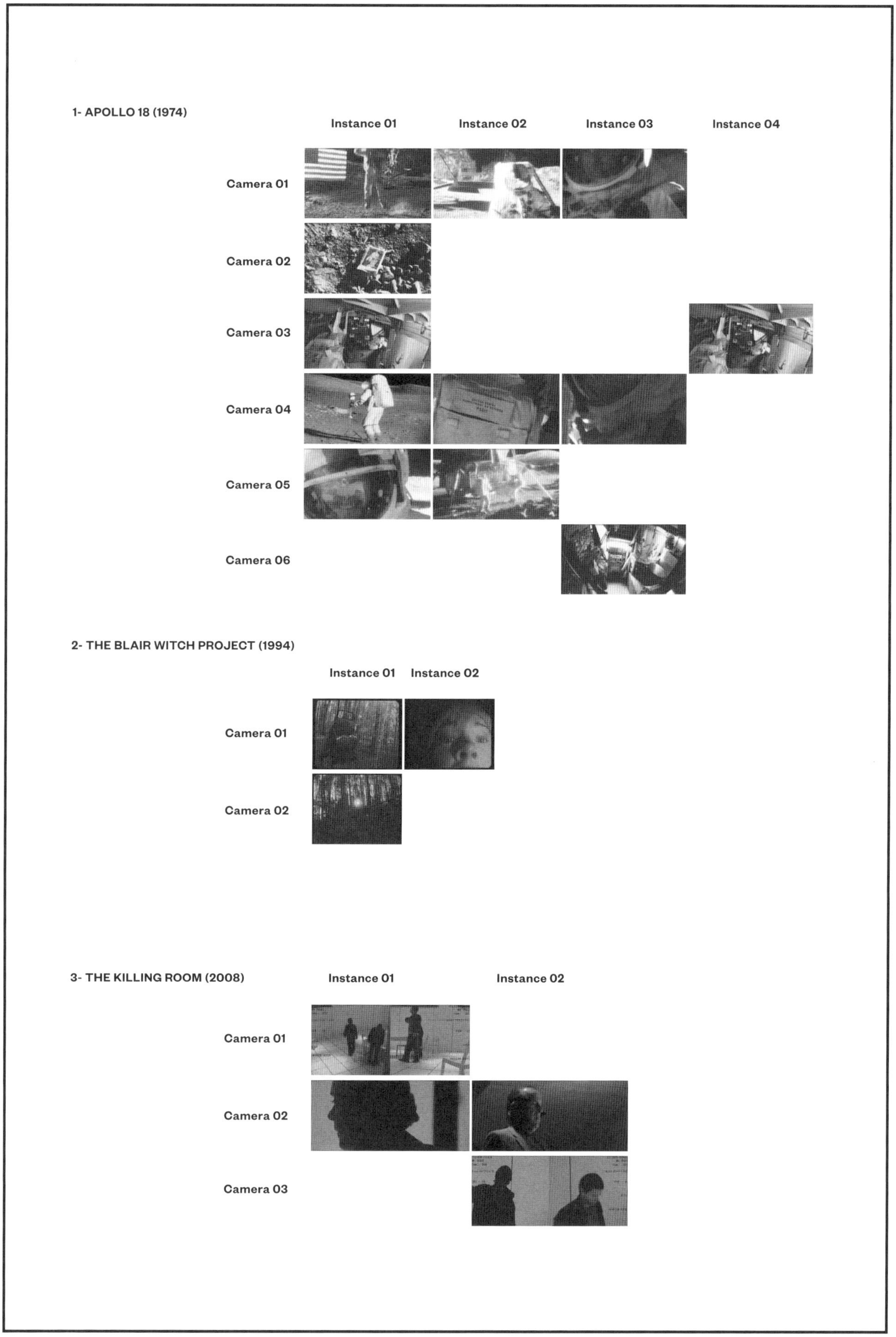

(02) Filmic analysis of three films' use of "found footage" strategies.
The number of cameras used for filming and the common distances
between the camera and subject were tracked.

Christos Bolos—Wilshire Theater

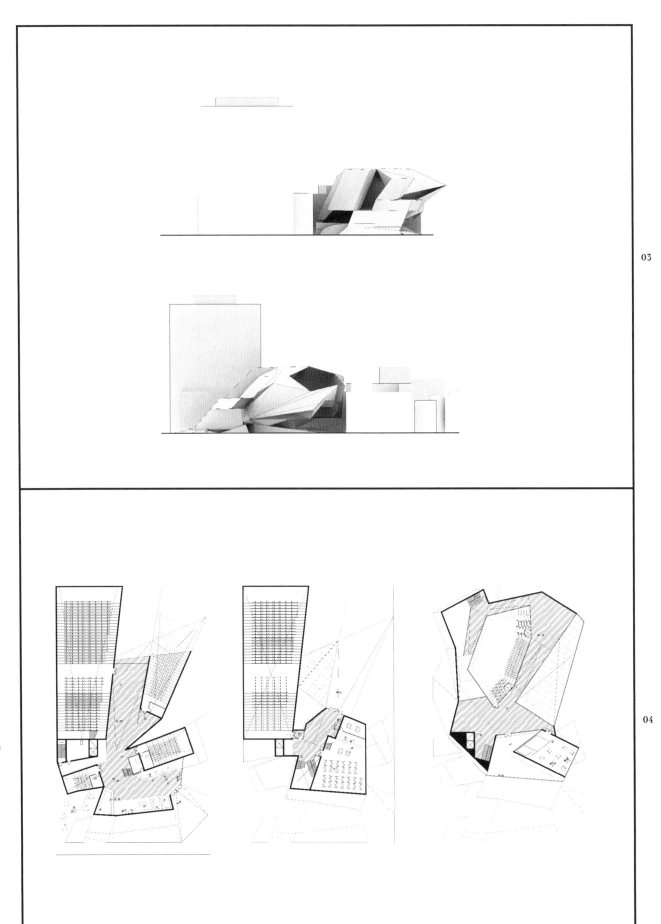

03

04

(03) Exterior elevations, showing the proposal from Wilshire
Boulevard and Virgil Avenue. (04) Floor plans, showing levels one,
two, and four. The entry, gift shop, and traditional film theaters
are located at level one. Level two consists of the film archive, and
level four contains the largest traditional theater, ideal for 70-milli-
meter film. On level four, the restaurant, outdoor patio, and the lower
level of the LCD theater are arranged around a central auditorium.

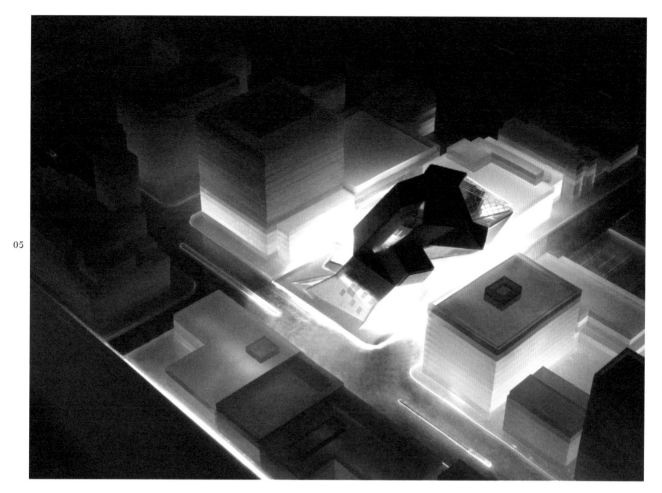

05

06

07

08

(05) Final model of the proposal, showing nighttime lighting array.
(06/07/08) Process model, showing the progression of geometric
manipulation performed on the original heptagonal form.

Christos Bolos—Wilshire Theater

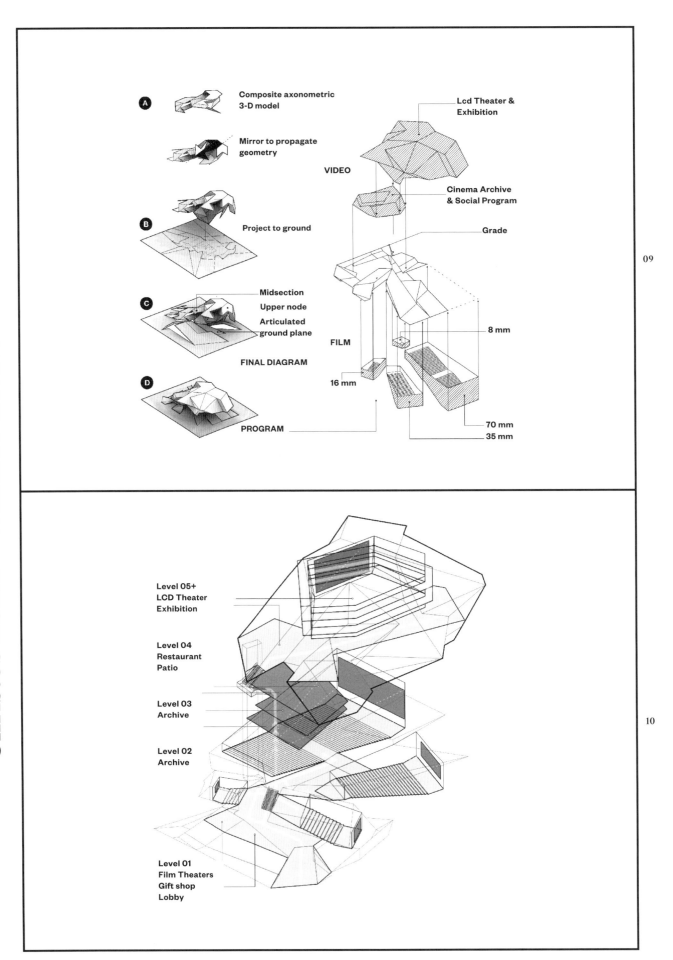

A — Composite axonometric 3-D model

Mirror to propagate geometry

B — Project to ground

C — Midsection
Upper node
Articulated ground plane

FINAL DIAGRAM

D — PROGRAM

Lcd Theater & Exhibition

VIDEO

Cinema Archive & Social Program

Grade

8 mm

FILM

16 mm

70 mm
35 mm

Level 05+
LCD Theater
Exhibition

Level 04
Restaurant
Patio

Level 03
Archive

Level 02
Archive

Level 01
Film Theaters
Gift shop
Lobby

(09) Composite axonometric diagram, showing the process of moving from the manipulated geometric form to the massing of the proposal. The geometry is mirrored and merged to the site to establish the form of the proposal, into which the various theater spaces are introduced.

(10) Circulation and organizational diagram, showing the relative disposition of theaters within the proposal. The circulation pattern runs between the theaters at the lower level and wraps around the large LCD-screen theater on level five.

(11) Interior view, showing the exhibition auditorium. The circulation ramp that wraps around the LCD-screen theater is seen at left. (12) Exterior view of the proposal, as seen from Wilshire Boulevard. (13) Interior view of the high-definition LCD-screen theater, as seen from the upper level.

Lang Wang—Wilshire Parallax

Moving from preliminary filmic analysis to architectural design, this project's aim is to create both audience space and observer space. This project makes a distinction between the observer and the audience. While traditional audience space fosters total, passive viewing, observer space offers a more subjective relationship with the film being viewed. In the project, film space and observer space are split and independent but meet each other in unexpected ways for the observer, positioned as a voyeur who is always hidden from the gaze of the film's audience. In one scenario, the observer peeks through holes and gaps in the architecture, seeing only a part of the space but remaining unaware of its totality. In another scenario, the observer witnesses multiple, overlapped spaces that are projected onto a translucent screen.

The proposal examines the possibilities of breaking from conventional cinema and moving toward multiple projections on various surfaces. The architecture dramatizes how different spaces interact with one another. By formally breaking the black box and focusing on the infusion, opening, and folding of surfaces, this proposal alters the typical spatial relationship of the visitors and creates a new interaction between the reality of life and the fantasy of film.

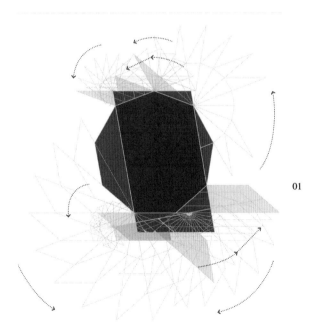

01

(01) Planar dissection diagram, showing the manipulation of geometry through fragmentation and rotation. This diagram was the basis of the visual manipulations of proposal's plans and sections.

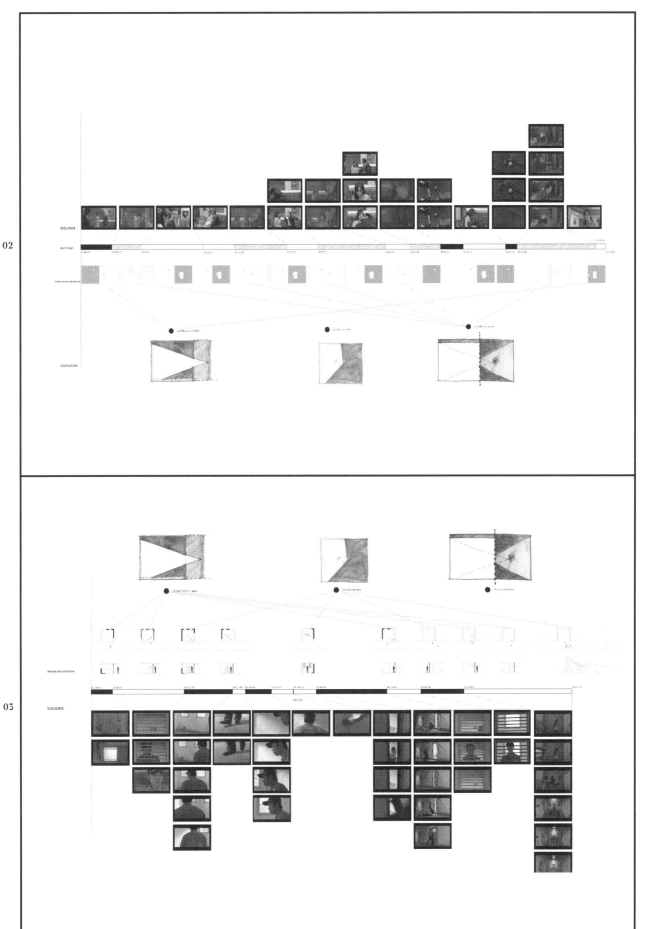

(02) Filmic analysis of the principles of voyeurism, charting the spatial relationship of the camera and its subject. Multiple voyeuristic relationships exist between the characters. Through mirroring, overlapping, and penetration, one space is split into different subspaces.

(03) The camera (and audience) participates in these scenes through first-person perspective. This relationship between the camera, a character, and a hidden character (the camera, the audience) informs the filmic analysis.

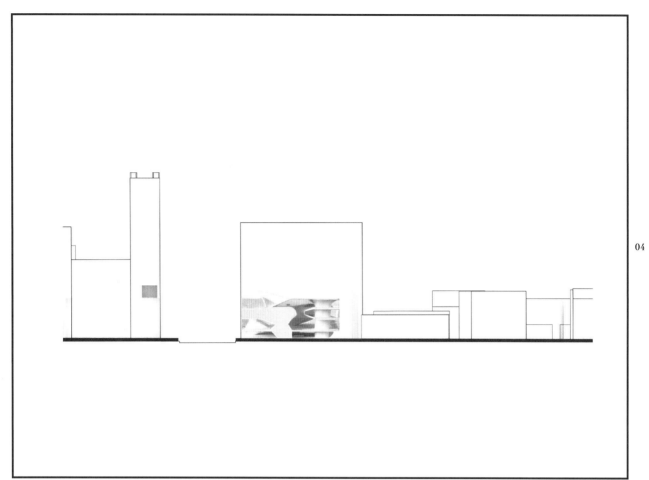

04

Lang Wang—Wilshire Parallax

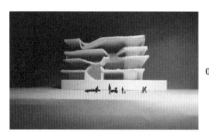

05

06

07

(04) East elevation, showing the facade along Virgil Avenue.
(05) Sectional model, showing the east side of the project. The
small theater is on the second level. (06/07) Details of the model.

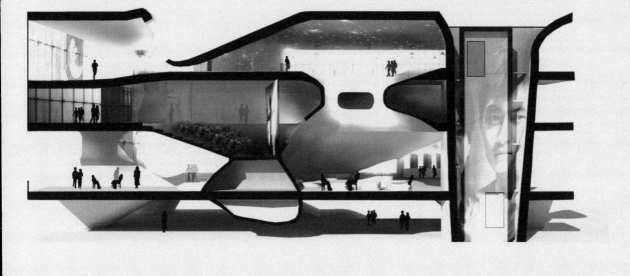

(08/09) Building section, cutting through the east end of the project
and showing the smaller of the two theater spaces and the fluid transition between floor plates. Building section, cutting through the center
of the large theater. The design employs stairwells, ceilings, floors,
and traditional screens as surfaces for projection. This blurs
the boundary between different spaces as well as that between reality
and imagination.

Amy DeDonato—Frozen Music

Using a filmic analysis and a dissection of geometric planes, this proposal for a new cinema house in Los Angeles investigates architecture's relationship to filmic technique. Studying the underlying structure of Alain Resnais' Last Year at Marienbad (1961) uncovered two distinct cinematographic techniques operating in opposition: the continuous tracking shot, or the continuous present, versus the jump-cut, or point of rupture. For the omniscient viewer, the entanglement of these two methods produces a radically distorted sense of time, conflating recollections of the past and imagined or dreamed events with scenes of the present.

For this cinema project, these two filmic techniques help to define an architectural strategy that animates the difference between spatial repetition (as a homogenous digital script) and spatial rupture or discontinuity (as an aberrant break within the building's formal system). If filmic representation is three-dimensional space represented on a flat, two-dimensional surface, the challenge was to translate a filmic idea into three-dimensional space itself. In order to establish a tangible relationship between the filmic and the architectural, further study examined the possibilities of space differentiated through single and multi-point projection. Formally, the spatial distinction manifests itself on the exterior of the building as a ruptured

black-box cinema. Spaces are released from the traditional constraint of the exterior envelope and exist in varying degrees of autonomy. Traditional, single-point projection spaces rely on a single surface for image display in a fixed direction. Multi-point projection, however, introduces the possibility of projection as volume, which alters the viewer's relationship to the image as he or she moves through space. While surface projection prescribes fixed or established relationships between the object and the viewer, volumetric projection does not rely on either a fixed point as a source or the visitor's experiencing the film from a single point. While the traditional cinema spaces repeat vertically throughout the building, volumetric projection spaces are interspersed throughout the building, offering new-media artists a great level of flexibility and indeterminacy.

The cinema is sited on a plinth at the corner of West Sixth Street and South Commonwealth Avenue, removed from the repetitious, large-scale structures of Wilshire Boulevard. The building's flat facade and its relationship with the ground plane reflect that of the Los Angeles County Superior Court. Positioned as a freestanding object-in-the-round, each of the cinema's facades projects a frozen snapshot of a cinema-house undergoing typological transformation.

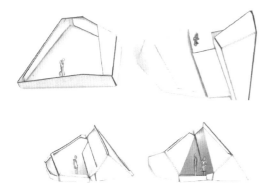 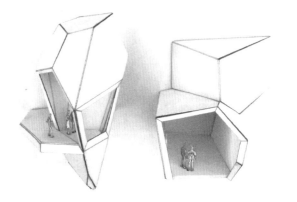

01

(01) Multi-point projection study model, exploring the possibility of projection as a volume rather than as a static, single plane.

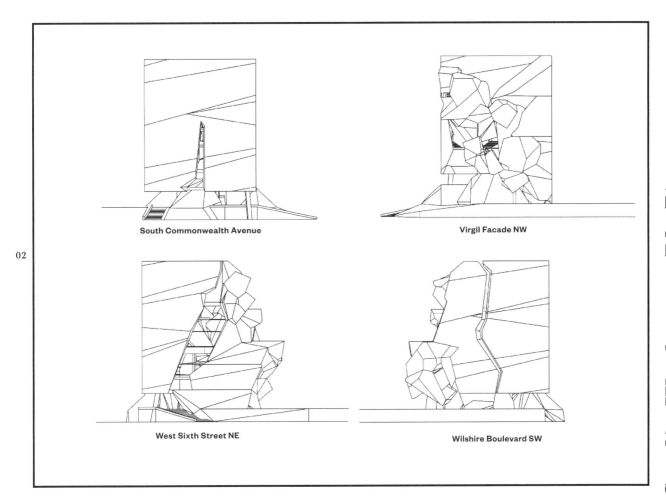

02

South Commonwealth Avenue

Virgil Facade NW

West Sixth Street NE

Wilshire Boulevard SW

03

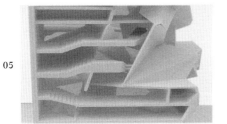

05

04

(02) Model/study of cinema elevations, showing the flat facades that face Wilshire Boulevard and the ruptured facades facing Virgil Avenue. The base plinth supports the "object-in-the-round" and its multi-point projection spaces above. (03) Site model viewed from Wilshire Boulevard. The flat facade is oriented toward the shift in the axis of Wilshire as it approaches downtown Los Angeles.

(04) View of the model in the context of Wilshire Boulevard. The mass breaks from the grid of the surrounding streets and buildings and presents differing levels of fragmentation on each facade.
(05) Sectional model, showing the variety of theater configurations. The massing ruptures as it approaches Virgil Avenue.

06

(06) Exterior view from the corner of West Sixth Street and South Commonwealth Avenue, showing the entry stair and ruptured facade.

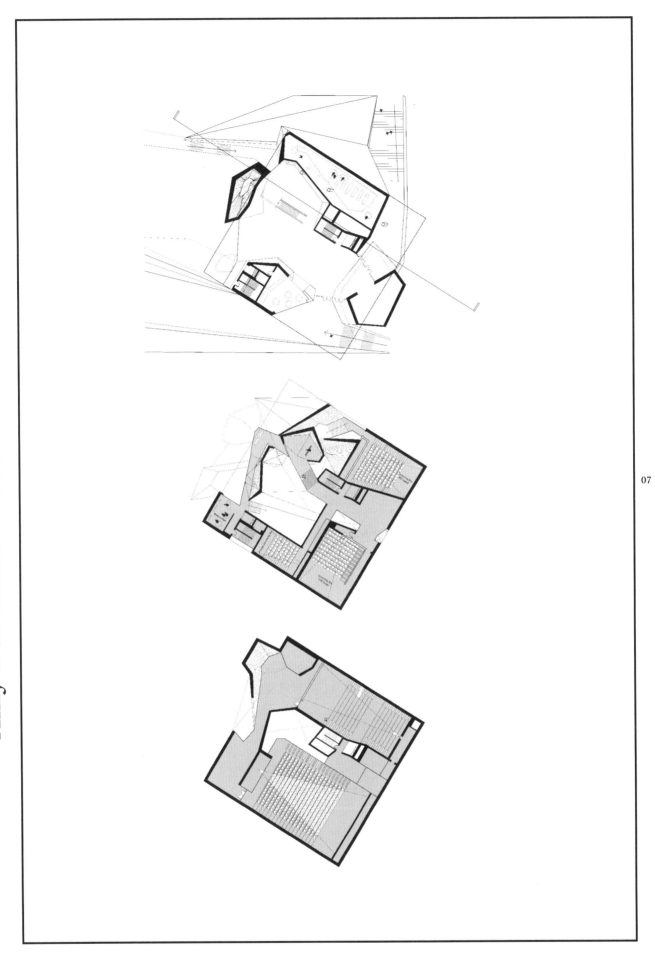

(07) Building plans, showing three principal levels of the project.
The building rests on a base plinth that supports the ruptured
black box above. Large, traditional theaters occupy the plinth,
and the immersive, multi-point projection spaces emerge on the
upper levels.

02—Tom Wiscombe, The Broad Redux

Interview with Tom Wiscombe

Tom Wiscombe discussed his work and his teaching with Nina Rappaport, prior to the beginning of the Yale studio.

Nina Rappaport: Since you started your Los Angeles–based firm Emergent in 1999, the form and structure of animal and natural elements has influenced your work. How has it changed specifically in the past few years from direct metaphors and analogies to the design of actual buildings?

Tom Wiscombe: I am less interested in the science of biology these days and have gotten more interested in the animals themselves as unique, specific things. Animals are quite strange when you examine them closely. They stand out from their context, even when attempting to camouflage themsleves, through fascinating figuration, shape, colors, patterns, and behaviors. Looking closely at good architecture is like looking at animals. You can't describe good architecture in terms of its contexts—it always exceeds its context. Look at the white Bengal tiger. Evolution is a terrible way to understand Bengal-tigerness. It is reductive, either downward into parts or upward into super-unities, as in concepts of ecology and so on. You can't draw forth buildings from information in general and certainly not from vague notions of nature or "the world." And, by the way, buildings don't evolve. That is why I have such a problem with contemporary architecture that is described in terms of the forces or processes that supposedly generated it and how architecture solved this or that problem. Animals don't solve problems; they just are. Architecture does not exist to solve problems, either, although, obviously, buildings do, to some extent. Architecture is about freedom, imagination, and mystery. Science is about knowledge. The two are incongruent. Certainly, when we talk about the discipline of architecture, we are talking about the humanities and not science.

How do you see the relationship between architecture and, on the other hand, nature and ecology in, for example, your Busan Opera House? Do you want to have a blurred boundary between the two? I notice you also don't talk about nature in terms of sustainability but in terms of form and structure. Where is that approach taking your work?

Yes, I am trying to achieve nuanced architectural effects by synthesizing different aspects of the natural world with things from contemporary culture, such as tattoos. I always try to put more than one thing into the mix, which keeps the products from being immediately consumable. I like the idea of the cross-genre architect who, nonetheless, operates within disciplinary boundaries. This is different than the "interdisciplinary" architect, which, I think, is problematic in the sense that it weakens any claim to expertise, which I wholeheartedly believe in.

I would also like to note, in the Busan project, the importance of the concept of a "near-figure"—that is, something that is neither abstract nor purely figural but somewhere in between. The near-figure is something that is very contemporary because it surpasses the problem of form versus shape, which has been a matter of debate for some time between Greg Lynn and Bob Somol and usually dealt with as discordant. Another angle to this project is the concept of an "implied outer shell," which definitely has environmental and urban implications, although they are not primary. The near-figures are the two theaters, which bulge out from what is really a giant delaminating surface. The outer shell, which is articulated by giant tattooed apertures, forms a buffer zone between inside and outside. The implied outer shell is a way of creating a loose spatial boundary in excess of the actual limit of the envelope. It creates a great deal of shade in a particularily hot environment, a kind of spatial micro-climate. Would I call this strategy sustainable? Maybe not in the conventional technical sense, but my answer is yes.

Earlier, you were looking at the structures and traceries of things like butterfly wings.

I still do. There is an amazing fish called the Mandarin fish that has multiple kinds of patterns on its skin, patterns which don't necessarily belong together, like stripes and spots. Sometimes the stripes follow structural pleats in the fins, but sometimes they spin off and run counterintuitively, free-form across the body. I love that. But we both know a fish is not architecture. The fish just keys off of a larger interest I have in exploring a dissonant tectonic relation between structure, skin, and surface articulation.

But is it simply inspiration or biomimicry?

I really don't want architecture that looks like something organic, like a creature. And I am not interested in "growing" buildings—in fact, I find that a very strange impulse. I shifted the branding of my office a few years ago because I don't want to be associated with what the word *emergent* has come to mean in our field. I still use it often in the office and in my writings—it is such a game-changing concept. But it started to be associated with the pseudo-scientific, rational computation front, and those who, as you say, are attempting to literally imitate natural processes to make architecture. My work is not about auto-generating anything; quite the opposite, it has a lot to do with craft. My new company name, Tom Wiscombe Architecture, allows me freedom to grow and speculate.

In terms of integrating a building's infrastructure with new materials, what do these materials allow you to

do with surface and structure, as well as the tracery that you have written about? Can these materials be harnessed in an organic way by peeling them back or using composites?

The idea that you can fuse any number of things into a very thin surface, which is something we can do with composites, is very exciting. Thin-film lighting, radiant heating and cooling, solar systems, and a number of other technologies can literally be pressed into the resin and fiber layup. Composites already fuse envelope and structure into surface, so why not push it to the next level? I like the idea of squishing and sedimenting rather than assembling things with hardware. Conceptually speaking, it's more like a Korean seafood pancake than a modern trabeated assembly. This is what I began referring to as "multi-materiality" a few years ago.

The important thing is that architects begin to lay out new tectonic theories appropriate to this new paradigm, what we might call the "polymer" paradigm. For instance, when you no longer get articulation for free from the gaps and seams between little pieces of mineral materials like bricks, sticks, or panels, what do you do then? I think the key will be in developing a whole new lexicon, which I am in the middle of doing. A couple of these are "metaseams," which are seams that do not index material ends or limits but, rather, create strange scale effects and fake breaks in continuity, and "supercomponents," which are giant chunks of building which can be delivered, fully integrated, by helicopter to construction sites without conventional delivery and sequencing methods.

How does that counter with your idea of thickened skins and inhabiting a poche or integrating the surface with the guts of architecture? In your earlier work and writings, you have talked about poche as an active space and not a solid, something we should operate within, along with the idea of delamination. How does that relate to the new idea of material flatness?

That is a great question. Although I am talking about surface thinness, I am very interested in what happens when you have multiple layers of surface, like an onion, and what can occur in the interstitial space. By delaminating layers, you can create pockets and volumetric effects out of the instrument of a very thin surface. This is the contemporary version of poche: everything is surface, rather than the classical version, which, of course, is literally uninhabitable because it consists of solid masonry. Poche is now like a parallel universe in the sense that it is right on the other side of a surface but may contain an entirely other world. One particular type of poche we are working on now is created when a near-figure is delaminated from a flat surface, and both surfaces are retained. Another kind that has been very useful is what we call a "liner," which is an interior surface that is completely free to either follow exterior building form or deviate from it, as in Baroque architecture. Liners, especially when loose-fit, can create mysterious spaces, like attics or basements, but they are particularly useful for building circulation. I am very interested in supressing building circulation in these kinds of spaces, including elevators, stairs, and escalators, which I associate with gratuitous displays of technology.

Is this how your concept of "surface to volume" gets constructed?

Yes. The idea of surface-to-volume form is that it is in a kind of dimensional middle ground. Think of something that is razor-sharp transforming into something that appears to be heavy and massive. Like a line being teased out of a volume and threatening to become a surface or a fist punching into a rubber sheet, which appears as mass on one side of the surface and as a hole or involution on the other. This formal interest emerged relatively organically, but I have now begun to build on it and write about it. I built a pavilion for a show at MOCA, Los Angeles, based on that idea, where a very thin surface transformed into what appeared to be heavy, massive objects on the interior.

How did your early experience with Wolf Prix evolve into the development of your own firm and inform your work?

I spent the better part of my early career working for Wolf and designing big projects. I feel a great connection to him and the work we did, and there is no question that certain approaches to massing and organization have influenced my own work. One is the idea of an aquarium, where figures are arranged inside a transparent container, as in the Dresden Cinema I did for him twenty years ago. With my work, though, the focus is more on how discrete objects can interface in a more complex way just short of fusing together. I like the idea of empathy, that objects could begin to empathize with one another, nestle into one another, even encase one another in strange ways. This way of working pays off in terms of near-figure formal effects and also the interstital spaces that are created, as in our National Center for Contemporary Arts, Moscow. The graphics dimension of my work, which I have referred to as tattoos, is also intimately tied to the formal

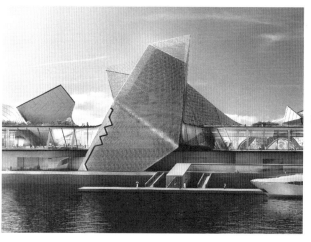

01

(01) Water-view detail from Kinmen Passenger Service Center, Kinmen Island, Taiwan

02

Interview with Tom Wiscombe

03

(02) Water view of Kinmen Passenger Service Center, Kinmen Island, Taiwan. (03) Street view from Kinmen Passenger Service Center, Kinmen Island, Taiwan. (04) Interior view of Kinmen Passenger Service Center, Kinmen Island, Taiwan.

effects I am after, which is something Wolf and I never explored in his office. There are other things, as well—for instance, my interest in visually suppressing circulation. Wolf prefers to turn pathways into independent spatial figures.

How do you engage projects with a scale similar to those you did with Coop Himmelb(l)au?

Well, yes, the idea is to get back into my comfort zone of doing large public projects. I just took second place in stage two of the Kinmen Port Terminal project in Taiwan—that is probably the closest I have come to date. I also worked with Thom Mayne recently as part of his joint design team on a competition for a massive ground-up university in Shenzhen for the Chinese University of Hong Kong. As much as I like to do speculative work, I have to admit I really enjoy addressing age-old disciplinary issues like silhouette, how a building hits the ground, interiority, and entry sequence. With big projects, the strategic and political angles are vexing and exciting.

Will those competitions in China be built? What has it been like working there?

A couple of years ago I was in Beijing and Shenyang every two weeks, trying to realize a pair of competition-winning projects—stadiums for the Chinese National Games. Winning a competition means something quite different in China than in the West, however. It is a messy process. But by doing a series of invited competitions, I began to meet people, and I met a developer who asked me to design a two-million-square-foot hotel in Beijing. I am still fully invested in working in China, and now I feel much more comfortable there and able to maneuver, to some degree. But things have changed there radically for Western architects recently. I get the feeling we are at the close of an era of architectural colonialism, which had to happen. There will be new ways into China, though. It is transforming itself at a radical pace.

SCI-Arc has become a real base for you. What will your Yale studio focus on? And how has teaching informed your creativity?

I don't know how I would have a practice without teaching. It is critical to have the chance to test things out and engage colleagues. My favorite thing is being surprised by something going on at school that fundamentally changes my way of thinking. At Yale, I will be working with the students on the idea of "figures in a sack," an idea related to the surface-to-volume project we spoke about, and include threads back to Kipnis' writings on the "sectional object," from 1993.

I plan to have the students look at some work by the Dutch artist Bart Hess, who is dealing with that subject in terms of the human body. We will also look at important architectural precedents like Nouvel and Starck's Tokyo Opera House competition entry (1986) and Bunshaft's Beinecke Rare Book and Manuscript Library (1963) at Yale. The goal is to build on a long trajectory 'things inside of things' in architecture.

What are you working on next?

Frankly, my first five-year plan is coming to a late close now. I wanted to speculate and try to locate something authentic to dwell on, work on. It has taken some time, but recently I am beginning to see things around the office that I know I could work on for a lifetime. This has pushed me to begin setting up a theoretical framework that compliments the work. I'm not interested in justifying the work, but thinking about it in parallel.

The project I am most excited about now is the Old Bank District Museum in downtown Los Angeles. It is Tom Gilmore's private art museum and my first major commission. It deals with my interest in discreteness, near-figuration, and so on. The site is beneath, inside of, and on top of four historical banking buildings. How to tie all the parts together into something we can understand as a museum is the question that intrigues me.

05

(05) Street view of National Center for Contemporary Arts, Moscow

(06) Aerial view of the Old Bank District Museum, Los Angeles

The Object Turn—Tom Wiscombe

Over the past twenty years, digital architecture has gone through two distinct periods, and it is on the verge of an uncertain third. This third period, depending on one's particular bent, is either "post-digital," as in the case of the recent interest in low-fidelity forms, or it is "meta-digital," as in "big data" computing. Regardless, we can now think of the digital in historical terms, rather than as something that is perpetually emerging or as one homogeneous mass of work, and take stock of its particular contribution to the long arc of architecture. Most important, we can begin to trace how the digital has created unprecedented speculation on new models of coherency in architecture, ranging from positions promoting total smoothness and relational ontologies to more recent positions promoting discreteness of things and more unexpected models of coherency.

From Relations to Objects

The first period of digital architecture, spanning the 1990s, was a time of experimentation in which digital tools opened up new ways of making form, representing form, and thinking about form in a design space free of the baggage of the "critical project" of the decade before. This period saw work on hybrid and relational forms, variable forms, "abstract machines," and evolutionary processes. Further, this work was driven not only by the availability of new tools from the entertainment industry but because of a strong resonance with the philosophy of Gilles Deleuze and its focus on multiplicities, intensive forces, and becoming. Analogies that enthralled architects included the rhizome, an open system of endless flows and connectivity, and the werewolf, a singular multiplicity with both hybrid formal and psychoanalytical dimensions. Lofting, the NURBS operation of sweeping surfaces between lines, seemed the perfect tool to connect and bridge between things in the world, be it a house and a ground or a chair and a wall. It became common for architects at the time to attempt to transform a building massing into its "other," as in the case of a building becoming landscape or to set up systems of intensive force fields in which architecture might spring forth from virtual resonances from the outside world. One proponent of this paradigm is Sanford Kwinter, who argued that form is best understood through its intensive relations, using the analogy of Conrad Waddington's "epigenetic landscape," a model of DNA expression visualized by a warped surface controlled from beneath by virtual puppetry wires. Through focus on generative processes, the architectural object became difficult to discuss on its own terms; one could describe it only as a bundle of relations or as one of many possible outcomes of sets of relations. Outcomes tended toward the smooth and topological and sometimes the entirely formless, as if waiting for more information from the outside to instantiate them and lock them into existence.

This period was extremely important for architecture in terms of the revitalization of form in architectural thinking and its effectiveness in swerving the discussion away from the inherent critical problems of both Post-Modernism and Deconstructivism, toward new models of coherency. Still, in retrospect, its ontological underpinnings of relation over object—exemplified in Stan Allen's essay "From Object to Field"—were rarely questioned, even as a new homogeneity began to arise. For instance, when we began to see this relational ontology appear as a way to imagine the city and large infrastructural projects, it became instantly obvious how too much coherence—even when based on the logic of "continuous variability"—might eliminate the possibility of any real heterogeneity. One of the key concepts of Deleuzian philosophy, that of "disjunctive synthesis," or assemblage, often seemed to fall away in favor of a subliminal desire for super-unification.

The second period of digital architecture, beginning after the turn of the century, continued and expanded allegiances to the relational paradigm of earlier work, but became more specifically focused on architectural effects, especially surface effects. These effects were primarily produced by novel ornamental and tectonic articulation, often involving surface discretization of some kind. This work was often characterized in terms of its intricacy, excess, or in terms of formal variability and fabrication intelligence, both offering relief from the monolithic and uncharacterized quality of much early digital work. The concept of "continuous variability" endured and was expanded upon, often assuming that difference emerged from a neutral or primitive state. The dominant model for this approach was the locally inflected surface, responding to a range of aesthetic, material, or contextual factors. Nevertheless, difference was often in degree, rather than in kind; no matter how much a surface was perturbed, it remained a deformation registered against the foil of a neutral state and never became a new thing.

During this period, digital modeling tools evolved from splines and lofts to polygons and subdivision surfaces, which suddenly allowed for almost unlimited control of formal features. The creative limits of a calculus-based uniformity of meshes and, associated with lofting operations, a directionality of surfaces evaporated. Designers could suddenly shift between resolutions, orientations, and levels of refinement within a single surface patch. Interest in fineness and discretization was underwritten, as well, by the appearance of scripting and software plug-ins that enabled control of large numbers of fine-grain components. It also should be noted that the new digital rendering algorithms, which appeared at the same time, made the production of surface effects convincing, at least in terms of representation. Work from this period includes projects produced using parametric tools to produce smooth gradients of panels or apertures linked to surface variation and much more elaborate surface inflections connected to a renewed interest in the Baroque. Supporting this work was a parallel discourse on "mass customization," or the ability to produce

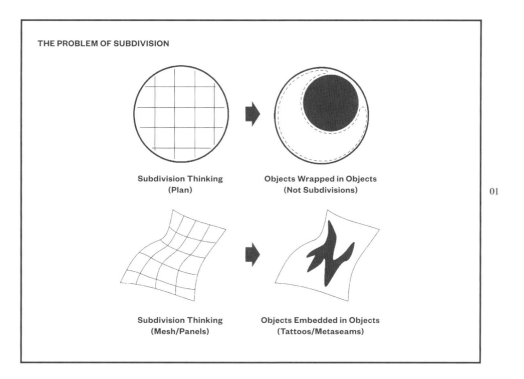

THE PROBLEM OF SUBDIVISION

Subdivision Thinking
(Plan)

Objects Wrapped in Objects
(Not Subdivisions)

Subdivision Thinking
(Mesh/Panels)

Objects Embedded in Objects
(Tattoos/Metaseams)

01

(01) The problem of subdivision

bespoke architectural components economically through the use of new digital fabrication tools, finally moving beyond Ford's production logic. Regardless of how it was framed—in terms of qualitative effects, techniques, or new advances in fabrication—this period was notable for its obsession with the surface and its continued alignment with Deleuzian models of the world.

Importantly, during this period, the abstract machines and diagrammatic emphasis of 1990s digital work were replaced by a will to elicit an affect in the viewing subject, thereby establishing another line of access in the overall relational paradigm. Architecture, rather than simply a result of abstract outside forces or contexts, became connected to the inner life of humans, essentially completing a giant super-unity of communication among all things in the world. This development deposited architecture into the realm of appearances and semiotics rather than the deep interiority of things-in-themselves. The implicit argument was familiar, recalling Kant's mind-world correlationist argument: Things exist only insofar as the human mind can access them. This assumption of the overarching value of social accessibility was and is the pinnacle of the relational ontology of architecture.

In the early 2010s, exhaustion with that model of coherency and access has started to become palpable in architectural discourse. The continuous-variation model of difference, which has since been consumed by practice, now looks all too familiar. And while the rhizome analogy continues to have traction in social and economic theories, it appears to have run its course in architecture. The idea that buildings are nodes in a super-unity of seamless communication now seems more like a utopian idea than something productive for architecture. It leaves out the importance of stoppages, tension, deferrals, edges, gaps, deep interiorities, and mystery in architecture.

This new ontological and epistemological framework does not require the literal correlation of all things, positing that architecture is at its best when it defies immediate access and consumption. It embraces the fundamental uniqueness of objects in the world, and how things can

enter into relations with one another without being defined or subsumed by those relations. Graham Harman, the object-oriented philosopher, notes how the object has been, in late-twentieth-century philosophy, consistently "undermined" and "overmined" by reductive science on the one hand, and by network and systems theory on the other. While it is problematic to equate a philosophical definition of "object" with what might constitute an architectural object, there is a clear parallel here in terms of the domination of relational ontologies over objecthood in contemporary architectural discourse.

While this turn toward objects could be misunderstood as a simplistic focus on gratuitous things torn from all context, in fact it has more to do with the focus shifting toward the alluring qualities of things-in-themselves while realizing their fundamental inaccessibility. Consider a Bengal tiger, Kubrick's monolith, a Mexican crystal cave, a blood-comb jellyfish: Each has an inaccessible interior life that is not reducible to bundles of external relations. For architecture, this does not mean that relations do not exist but, rather, that architectural entities might relate at a distance without literally flowing into or becoming one another. In any case, architecture would cease to be a hollow conduit of flows and, instead, become a nesting of objects within objects. This model points to a strange form of coherence in architecture, which theorist John McMorrough has spoken about as the space "between collage and emergence," where objects simultaneously retain discreteness but enter into relations to produce novel entities.

A brilliant analogy of this new middle ground is to be found in the artist Mike Kelley's *Deodorized Central Mass with Satellites* (1991–99), which involves collections of colorful stuffed animals tied together into bizarre but somehow coherent spheroid masses in which each toy is visible and participates in the whole but is not subsumed by the whole. A new object is produced that is not entirely distinct from each part. In his appreciation of the writings of H.P. Lovecraft, Harman uses the term "the general outline" to describe these entities that can neither be

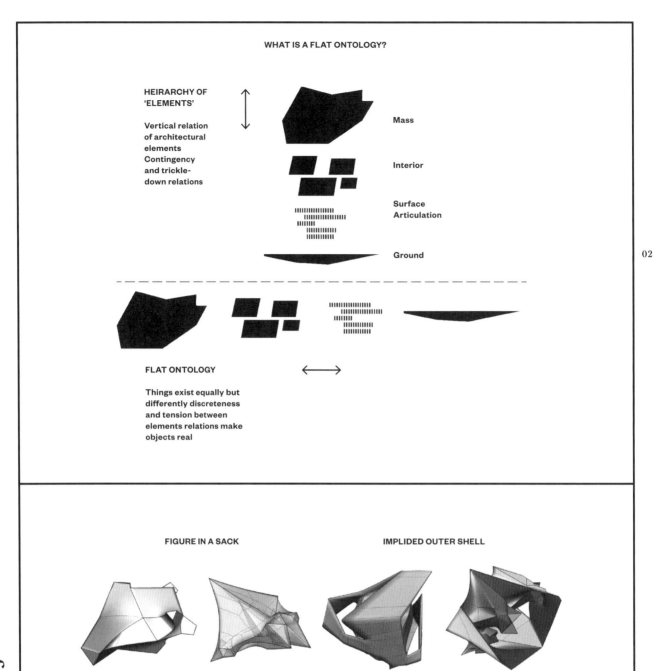

WHAT IS A FLAT ONTOLOGY?

HEIRARCHY OF 'ELEMENTS'

Vertical relation of architectural elements Contingency and trickle-down relations

Mass

Interior

Surface Articulation

Ground

02

FLAT ONTOLOGY

Things exist equally but differently discreteness and tension between elements relations make objects real

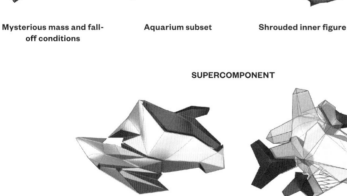

FIGURE IN A SACK

Mysterious mass and fall-off conditions

Aquarium subset

IMPLIDED OUTER SHELL

Shrouded inner figure

Simultaneity of inner and outer silhouette

03

SUPERCOMPONENT

Pressed in from outside

Inside and outside the container

(02) Flat ontology (03) Figure in a sack, implied outer shell, supercomponent

reduced to their parts nor fully explained as new things. Something that has a "general outline" can be described, at best, through association and metaphor, remaining otherwise inaccessible.

From Part to Whole to a Flat Ontology of Objects

The recovery of the object in architectural thinking has interesting repercussions on the discourse of part-to-whole relations. Part-to-whole in architecture is deeply rooted in Classical composition, which seeks to promote balance between the parts of a harmonious whole, as in a column base, shaft, and capital. This approach assumes that the parts of a whole are at the service of the whole, suggesting there is an innate hierarchy to the way things exist in the world. But what if there were only litanies of whole objects on a flat ontological plane?

Levi Bryant considers such a conundrum in his discussion of "strange mereologies," which describes a state in which objects can be autonomous but also enter into relations with one another to create a new object. This world is constituted by alliances and empathies of ontologically equal but radically different things, not a world of hierarchies or subdivisions. A flat ontological model forces a reevaluation of architecture's elements, which we may unwittingly place into hierarchies, such as building massing, surface articulation, structure, interiority, and ground. What if each of these elements was treated as an autonomous whole that, nonetheless, relate in such a way as to produce a new object?

So, what is the repertoire of this new architecture? First of all, the language of smoothness, endlessness, difference and repetition, becoming, landscape-buildings, smooth gradients, and total alignment of systems and subsystems would need to be replaced by a more abrupt terminology, such as chunks, strong silhouette, edge, separation, hovering, gaps, joints, nesting, embedding, interstitial space, and so on. The goal would not be to revert to Deconstructivism or collage by breaking things apart or celebrating disjunction but, rather, to create visual distinction of architectural elements and nuanced, tension-filled spaces between those elements. The results might include objects that are nestled into or wrap around one another, objects fully contained by other objects, and so on. Whatever the case, the critical factor would be that objects should not fuse together and lose their distinct character or become otherwise generalized. Harman theorizes how things that do not have direct access to one another can still "brush up" on one another. Perhaps the architectural equivalence of this would be Sylvia Lavin's concept of "kissing," in which bodies interact yet retain their discreteness.

Consider the radical difference between an owl and an aircraft carrier: one is giant, synthetic, monotone, and cavernous, while the other is tiny, variegated, and alive. We could of course imagine fusing the two together into a hybrid form, but a more contemporary move might be to retain their specificity and distinction yet nestle them into one another, creating a strange and unresolved new object. This new object might produce multiple associations, depending on the angle of view, the orientation of the elements, and the degree to which their individual silhouettes are retained or obscured in the arrangement. In architecture, the objects we deal with may not be so present to us as an owl or an aircraft carrier because, for so long, we have generalized things by reducing them to sets of relations. We talk about envelope as dependent on structure or building massing that emerges from local context or ground in response to natural flows, but none of this is, ipso facto, real. Peeling back the layers of relational thinking is actually quite a task because so many relations have been reified over the past twenty years of architecture.

There are still many pitfalls and angles to this new, still fragile direction in architecture to make definitive claims about its viability. It will no doubt be important to avoid turning philosophy into a set of instructions for architecture, as Richard Rorty warns. Language, as always, will be crucial, and any literal co-option of terms from philosophy should be met with skepticism; the definition of what constitutes an architectural "object" will clearly be front and center in the coming years. Coming to terms with the subject of autonomy will be imperative as well, since that particular discourse has already been established in a different time by a different generation with different goals. Finally, the discussion of "objects" must be broadened to include issues beyond aesthetics, ontology, and epistemology to include issues of function, typology, and technology. Only then will it be robust enough to meaningfully counter the entrenched relational paradigm in architecture.

Figures in a Sack: Studio Brief

"The two major sectional themes of DeFormation began to emerge. First, as far as possible, the section space of the building should not be congruent with the internal space implied by the monolith. Secondly, wherever possible, residual, interstitial, and other artifactual spaces should be emphasized over primary space. Because the box-within-a-box section is effective at producing both of these effects, it is often the tactic of choice, though by no means the only one possible." —Jeffrey Kipnis, "Towards a New Architecture" in *Folding in Architecture, AD* (1993), p. 46.

"[I struggle to give my sculpture] a sense that the form is pressing from inside, trying to burst or trying to give off the strength from inside itself, rather than having something which is just shaped from outside and stopped. Try clenching your fist and seeing your knuckles pushing through the skin, and you will see what I mean." —Henry Moore

Our studio agenda was focused on objects inside other objects, or, more specifically, nesting strong figures inside of loose outer sacks. Building on the box-in-a-box problem, also known as the the "sectional object" as adumbrated by Jeffrey Kipnis in his canonical essay "Towards a New Architecture," this studio explored new, contemporary relationships between container and contained. Rather than characterizing the relationship between inner figure and outer enclosure as "incongruous," we presumed from the beginning that this relationship could be more intimate and complex, while still maintaining discreteness of elements. In order to achieve this, it was important for us to move beyond the polarizing discourse of the last ten years concerning form and shape—that is, that form is about flow and coherence and shape is about contour and legibility, and that the two are mutually exclusive. We chose a third path, that of near-figuration, where the inner figure is sometimes revealed and sometimes obscured through its interaction with the outer form. Ultimately, our goal was to give glimpses of a mysterious interior world that is just out of reach.

The degree of looseness or tightness of the outer skin around figures created void spaces and formal features similar to those that occur when you push your fist through a rubber sheet or shrink-wrap an aggregation of crystals. One of our most important analogies was the exquisite *STRP Mutant* series by the artist Bart Hess, in which human figures are enveloped in a polymer sack, revealing particular features, hiding others. This was a perfect model for how a strange and coherent third object could be created without literally fusing figure and sack together. Multilayer sacks with internal liners were used to create further mystery and deferrals of interiority, where interstitial spaces could begin to form not only between figure and sack, but between sack, liner, and figure.

The fluctuating relation of figure and sack was enhanced by the introduction of strong graphic figuration. Tattooing was explored in terms of its capacity to either enhance underlying formal features or obfuscate them. The relation of tattoos to soft and hard form, edge conditions, cusps, apertures, and transitions between opaque and transparent materials was crucial. Nevertheless, tattoo drawings were also studied on their own terms, as discrete entities with their own internal rules and figuration. The interface of mass-object and drawing-object generated a productive feedback in terms of creating unexpected readings and associations in projects. In terms of technique, the intention was to engage the contemporary shift from untethered digital modeling in a single software environment to exploring custom digital workflows that allowed for issues of material behavior as well as drawing techniques to infiltrate the design object.

Building Project: The Broad Redux

The building project was a redesign of Diller Scofidio + Renfro's Broad Museum (2013), located adjacent to Frank Gehry's Disney Concert Hall on Grand Avenue in downtown Los Angeles. That project, as conceived by Eli Broad, is a Schaulager type in which the storage of the museum becomes part of the public gallery space. This organization lends itself to the figure-in-a-sack model and provided a perfect opportunity to test the studio agenda.

Students were asked to frame their projects in relation to the Disney Concert Hall in terms of extroversion versus interior sectional space, as well as in relation to the litany of architectural precedents that have contributed to the sectional object problem for the past twenty years. Examples of this tendency included Bunshaft's Beinecke Rare Book and Manuscript Library on the Yale Campus, Eisenman's Carnegie Mellon Research Institute, Nouvel and Starck's Tokyo Opera House competition entry, Shirdel's Nara Convention Center competition entry, OMA's Seattle Public Library, Prix's UFA Cinema Center, Herzog and De Meuron's Tokyo Prada, and Tschumi's Le Fresnoy, among many others.

Studio Work

Model 1: Figure in a Sack

This set of projects—from students Jacqueline Ho, Sarah Gill, Dino Kiratzidis, Peter Logan, and Jing Liu—were based on building upon the box-in-a-box problem, exemplified by the Yale Beinecke Rare Book and Manuscript Library and discussed by Jeffrey Kipnis in "Towards a New Architecture." To build on that problem, the students introduced complex formal relationships between container and contained in which an inner figure might become partially visible by pressing into an outer enclosure. This strategy produced a sense of mystery: the figure is never fully present but revealed only partially and indirectly. The quality and variety of interstitial spaces between inner figure and outer sack—the degree of tight and loose fit—was critical to this investigation. Simple offsets or lack of physical interaction between container and contained were avoided. In addition, a graphic layer was used to either emphasize or de-emphasize certain formal inflections and increase the mystery of the object.

Note: As mentioned, two different "models" emerged in the studio work: the figure in a sack and the implied outer shell.

Here, the term *model* refers to a speculative construction that holds in tension both formal and organizational properties. Therefore, a model is neither a diagram, which gives pragmatic organization primacy over form, nor a purely formal device, which gives primacy to the aesthetic. In this way, models can bridge what is often a divide in architecture between the conceptual and the visceral.

Jacqueline Ho—Black and Wight

This proposal investigates the implications of an invisible force applied to incongruent figures and mass and the ability of a graphic tattoo to enhance massing morphology while maintaining its own character. The project focuses on articulation in both the mass and the tattoo by exploring intricate and ambiguous language—smooth, spiky, faceted, and soft, all at the same time. This confluence of forms produces a type of strangeness that can be seen in the treatment of volume from monumental exterior to cavernous interior; in the layering of skins, tattoos, and embedded figures, and in the urban gesture to the corner that mimics its eccentric neighbor.

The program is a reenvisioning of the Broad Museum in Los Angeles. Two idiosyncratic inner figures house the art storage, auditorium, and administrative wing. These elements are enveloped by an outer membrane, and the tension among them is acted out in the massing morphology. A second membrane is introduced on the interior, lining the interstitial space between the figures and the outer skin. Finally, the entire building is nestled into an urban plaza, and all the energy of plaza is focused on the corner: visitors can travel through the exterior sculpture plaza, under the looming figure above, and into the cavernous gallery within.

The tattoo morphs with the outer skin due to pressure created by the inner figures. This organization orients the visitor toward the public front of the project, where the inner figures push out from within, pulling the skin so thin that black turns to white and cracks begin to appear. The goal was to allow the tattoo to track with mass inflections without losing its features in subservience, retaining a character of its own.

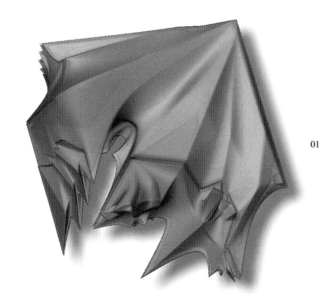

01

(01) This translucent digital model, describing the behavior of the outer skin. This skin mimics an elastic membrane that is veiled over sharp objects, then pulled in the opposite direction and inflated from within, resulting in pleats, folds, and wrinkles in the surfaces.

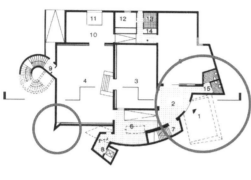

Frank Gehry's Vitra

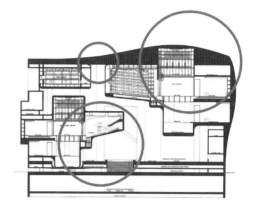

Jean Nouvel and Philippe Starck's Tokyo Opera House

02

03

(02) Frank Gehry's Vitra Museum and Jean Nouvel and Philippe Starck's Tokyo Opera House proposals were influential precedents for this project's exploration of the tension between inner figures and outer skin. (03) The urban gesture brings another element of strangeness to the project, focusing the energy on the northeast corner to mimic its eccentric neighbor, Frank Gehry's Walt Disney Concert Hall.

Box-in-a-box challenge

(04) Early box-in-a-box diagrams, exploring the possible relationships between object and enclosure, congruent and incongruent, tightness and looseness, intensity and blankness. (05) To generate the tattooed surface, a feedback loop was established between two- and three-dimensional techniques. By repeatedly transposing flattened patterns over volumetric forms, a level of predictability was established that allowed for precise development of the pattern while maintaining a degree of indeterminacy.

06

07

08

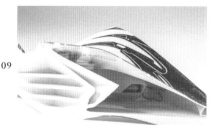

09

(06) The tattooed surface has been designed to accentuate the topography of the outer surface while retaining its own identity. Both an integral component of the form and independent of it, the tattoo was developed by the same rules as the building mass but intended to fulfill different needs. (07) Aerial view, showing the full context of the project, including the result of the tattoo investigation and the relationship between figure and ground. The northeast corner of the site includes access to an exterior plaza, which has been depressed into the ground at the moment of maximum surface articulation. (08) An earlier study, exploring the balance of intensity and calmness as played out in the action of forces on the outer skin. (09) A section through one of the inner figures reveals the tense relationship between figure and outer skin. An intestinal volume is the result of this relationship, and a second membrane helps to define it.

Sarah Gill—Bursting at the Seams

This proposal seeks to build upon the box-in-a-box problem by mixing precedents to create a layered interior that breaks through to the exterior.

In Ronchamp, one observes the use of incomplete lines to imply bounded volumes that are not fully enclosed. This strategy, when employed with greater density, produces labyrinthine or onion like layered spaces that allow for fluid transition from one to another. These indeterminate, fussy spaces act as a foil to the large hall and are meant to invoke a vastness of interior. Within the grand hall spaces, figures are suspended from the ceiling, extending dramatically down into the space. In their uses as circulation points, these hanging objects reference Prix's UFA Cinema.

On the exterior, the figure is indexed only by a seam near the Disney Concert Hall. Yet, as this seam travels west across the building, it widens and tears to finally reveal the crystalline figure within. This continuous seam allows for daylighting from the roof and sides as well as functioning as a series of entry points for the public and staff. It creates a rippling on the roof that, in turn, reflects the layered interior spaces. At the site, the tattoo is used primarily on the exterior, where the figures emerge, simultaneously highlighting this condition while confusing the boundary between sack and figure.

01

(01) Figures are suspended from the ceiling and used as circulation points, extending dramatically down into the space.

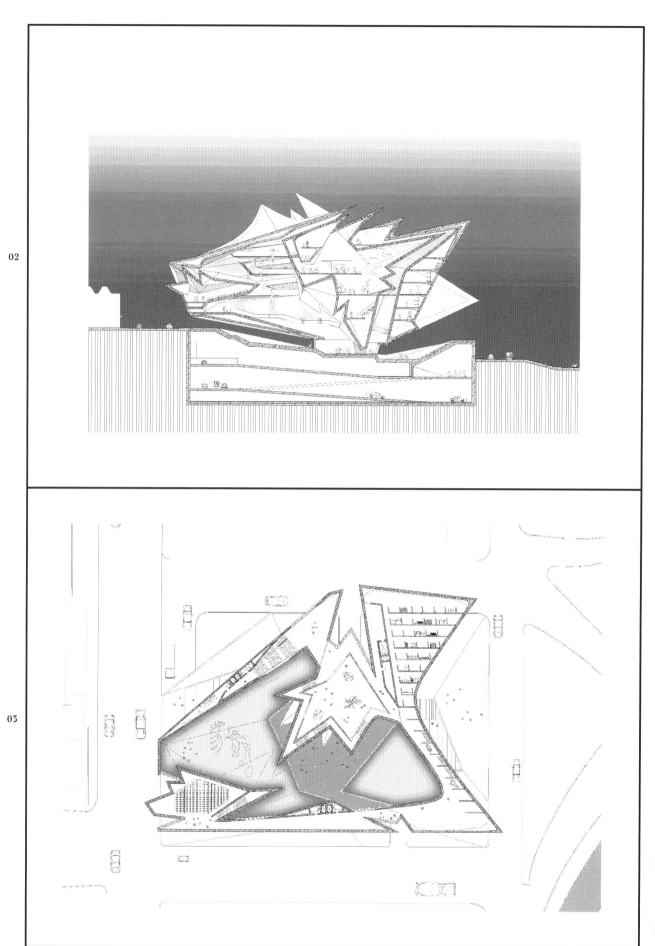

02

03

(02) Visitors enter the building by emerging into the multistory great-hall spaces, in which the layering of spaces is implicit, if not completely revealed. The section clarifies the distribution of program and circulation within the thickness and layering of walls. (03) This plan describes the techniques employed to blur the boundaries between intricate figures and the smooth outer skin. The perimeter is lined with program and circulation spaces, expressed as a gradually thickened wall into which crystalline figures are embedded. The shaded area demarcates the vast exhibition hall, which serves as a foil to the densely layered but fluid labyrinth of spaces.

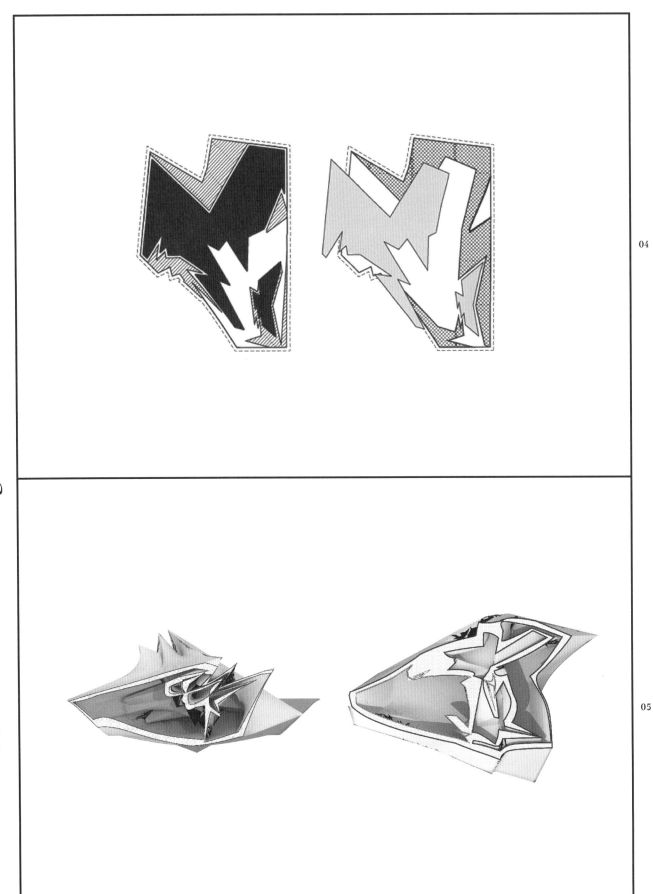

(04/05) Early sections of the project illustrate the emerging
crystalline form within.

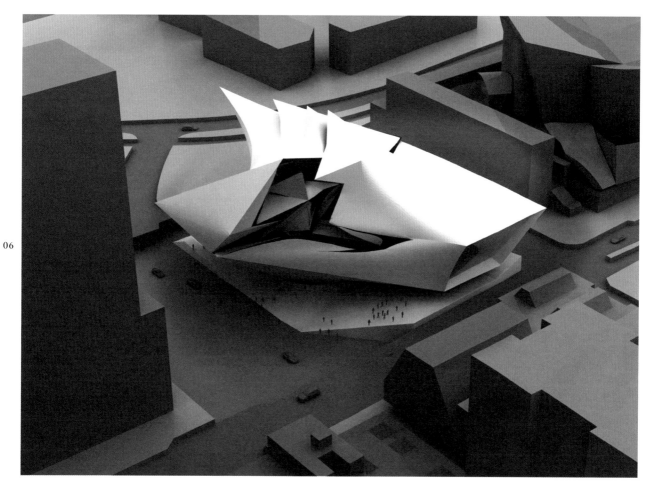

06

—Tom Wiscombe, The Broad Redux—The Studio Work—pp. 94–95

07

08

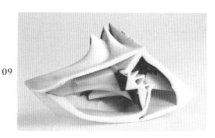

09

(06) With references to Ronchamp and UFA Cinema, the project builds upon the box-in-a-box problem by creating a layered, intricate interior that breaks through to the exterior, as seen in this rendering. (07/08) The smooth blank exterior is juxtaposed with the bursting of color and articulation at the seams, revealing an intensity within. (09) An earlier study, showing development of the exterior relative to the figure(s) within, gradually approaching a crescendo.

Dino Kiratzidis—Nested Space

Appropriating the formal organization of a (mutant) Russian doll, this project is conceived as a series of nested figures. Unlike the Russian doll, the figures are not given a consistent offset but are sometimes fused and, at other times, pull away from each other to accommodate various program functions. When this formal strategy is put into play with the given program of a museum, which, in this case, comprises a large public exhibit and a large visible storage vault, the system allows for the development of spaces as a gradient in four layers: from the most "internal" private spaces of the museum vault, which are thermal-conditioned, acoustically sealed, and artificially lit, to the most "external" spaces, which are public, unconditioned, and naturally lit.

The idea of an architectural tattoo is explored as a strategy to visually and tectonically break up the external layer into components. Like Frank Lloyd Wright's concrete-block houses, in which material is articulated through a range of relief patterns that, ultimately, punch through to become apertures, the tattoo here is manifested as a relief in parts and as an aperture for the spaces in which natural light is desired.

New developments in 3-D printing technology were used to develop the project. Compared to older paradigms of 3-D printing, which have tended to limit the output to a single smooth, off-white surface, the large-scale, multicolored 3-D prints produced for this project suggest a more heterogeneous tectonic assemblage and new ways of breaking up a complex surface in terms of both aperture and materials. In this way, this studio shows the capacity for rapid prototyping to assist in the development of new tectonic languages in digital design.

01

(01) In this view, the tattoo is an artistic and tectonic expression of a complex, sculptural skin.

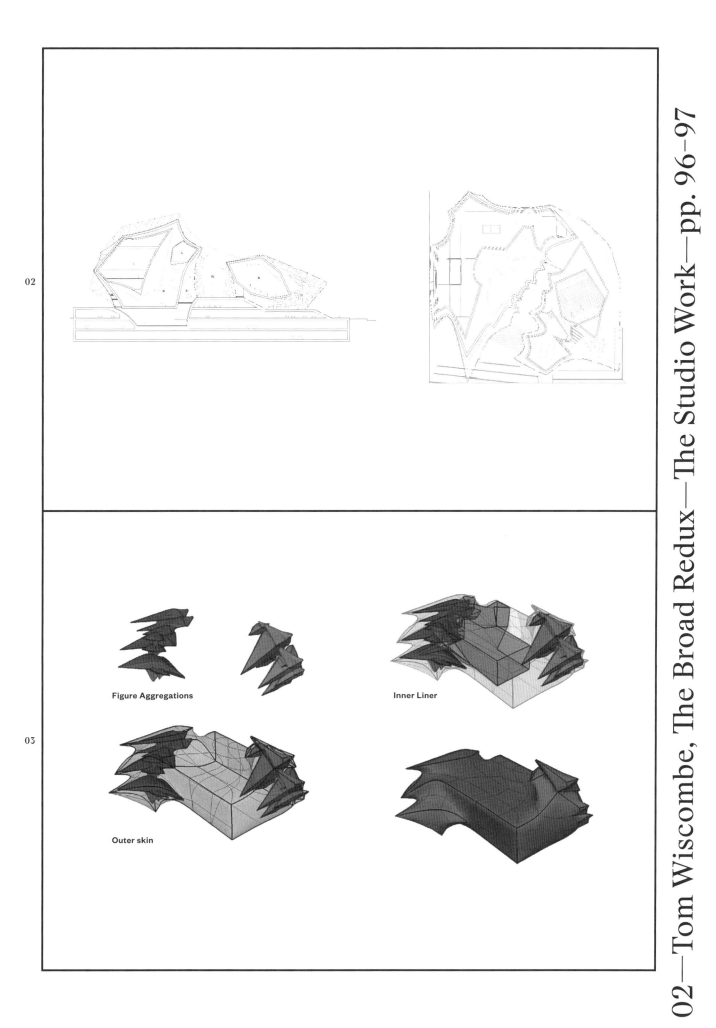

02

03

Figure Aggregations

Inner Liner

Outer skin

(02) Private and semi-public spaces, fully enclosed and conditioned, sit within an envelope that describes the public and external spaces, demonstrating the concept of nested figures. (03) These diagrams show the development and origins of the nested-figure concept.

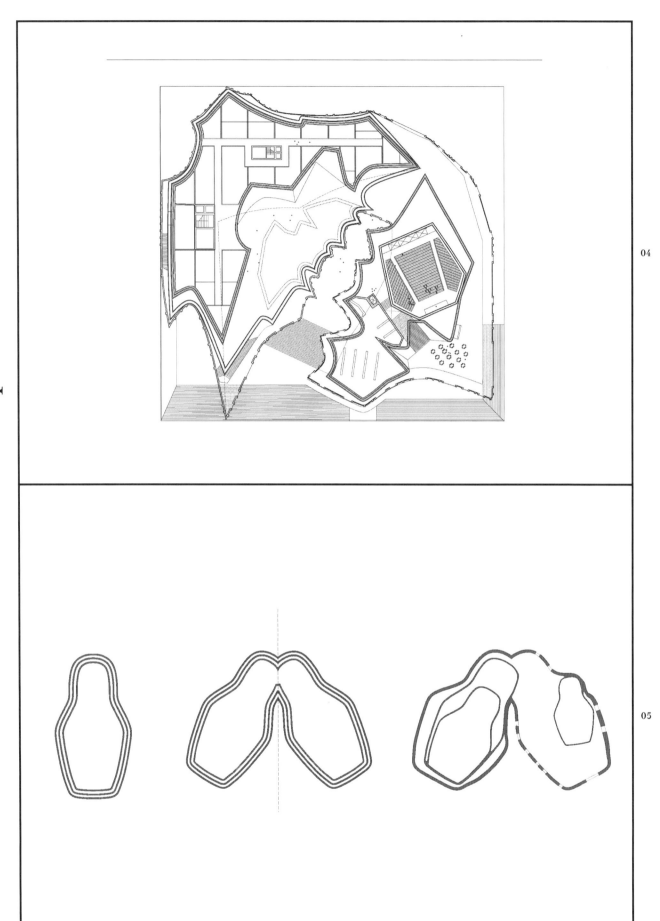

(04) This image shows the stepped entry plaza as well as the differentiation between porous exterior envelope and solid interior figures. The residual space between the inner and outer volumes is designed to include indeterminate programs and circulation. Moments like this within the project reveal the explosive language of figures nested inside figures. (05) The complexity of nested figures arises from disrupting the congruent offset geometry implicit in the Russian doll form. By pushing an inner figure against an outer figure, new forms and relationships emerge.

06

07

08

09

(06) The tattoo transitions from surface treatment to punctuations within the surface itself, giving rise to the dialectic and causal relationship between the tattoo and the envelope. (07) In this view, the tattoo is applied to give accent, relief, and character to the exterior envelope. (08) The C-shape plan form of the building creates an exterior public plaza. Raised above the level of the street, this plaza forms the entry into the building and a prominent place for the display of art and gathering of people. (09) This study model shows the development of the tattoo in relation to the outer envelope. The scale like texture of the tattoo is a first attempt at marrying surface with texture and creating a language of relief.

Peter Logan—Monster in a Box

Philip Johnson's glass house is an example of an incongruous figure within a regularized box, whereas the Beinecke Library displays a simple offset with little incongruity between figure and shell. A third model can be seen in Diller Scofidio + Renfro's Broad Museum design, in which a complex figure fits within a normative box. This project attempts to evolve the box-in-a-box concept by starting with a figural space— the "monster"—that is inserted into a generic box and exploring the tension generated as the monster begins to express itself outside the box.

A system of gradients developed as a strategy for articulating the outer shell, the internal figures, and the tattoo. The building retains its orthogonal edges adjacent the Disney Concert Hall, while the monster gradually stretches and deforms the outer skin toward the opposite end of the building. The outer skin takes on a character of the monster within as well. Sectional lines interpolated from the inner figure are projected onto the building's exterior. As the graphic rhythm approach the regularized box, the tattoo dissipates accordingly to mimic the taming of the geometry. The tattoo allows for three-dimensional relief and provides apertures where natural light is desirable.

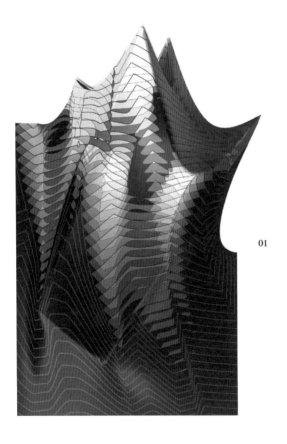

01

(01) The final tattoo enhances the tension between monster and box with a carefully calibrated gradient of color and contours.

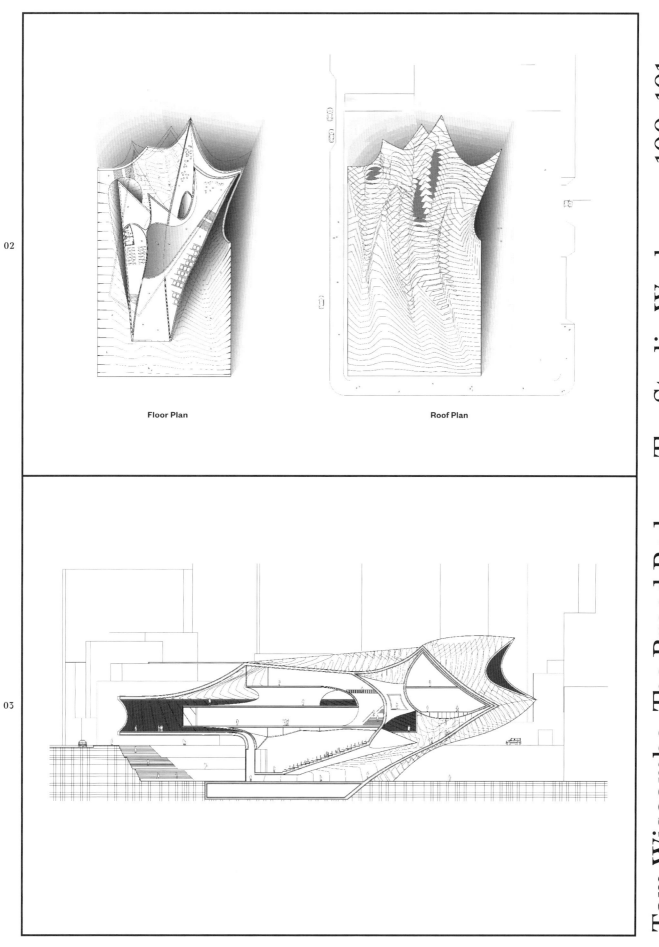

02

Floor Plan

Roof Plan

03

(02) The upper-level plan, describing the figural object wrestling against a Euclidian rectangle. The roof plan describes a more integral relationship, wherein the distinction between monster and box is less clearly delineated, resulting in a rich tension in both tattoo and underlying form. (03) The building retains its orthogonal edges adjacent to the Disney Concert Hall to the left, while the monster gradually stretches and deforms the outer skin toward the opposite end of the building. Visitors experience this tension in the varied interstitial spaces between the inner figures and outer skin.

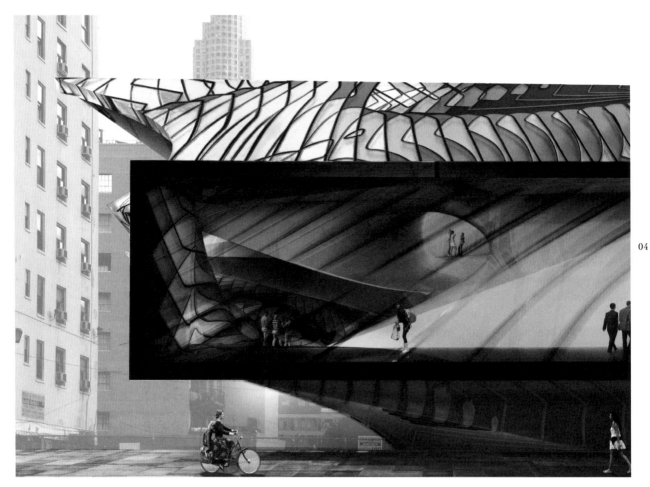

04

Peter Logan—Monster in a Box

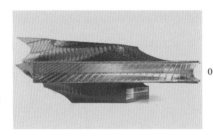

05

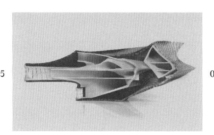

06

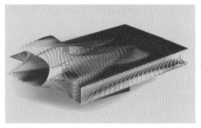

07

(04) A rendering of the museum from Grand Avenue, with views into the building and its activity through the highly articulated glazed facade. The role of the tattoo goes beyond graphic expression, providing a framework for structural components, delineating panel joints, and differentiating materials. (05) View from Grand Avenue, illustrating the volumetric contrast between the box and the morphology of the monster. (06) A longitudinal cut through the building reveals the relationship between the inner figures and outer skin, which is sometimes incongruent. The building interior has also been given its own gradient tattoo, allowing for alternative surface articulation within the building, rather than on the exterior. This differentiation further allows the interstitial space between the inner figures and outer skin to be legible. (07) View of the monster, facing the southwest. The tattoo and color gradient become more vibrant.

Jing Liu—Figural Feedback

This project explores surface-to-volume transformations to create complex architectural effects by crossing back and forth between 2-D and 3-D extended formations. A primary inspiration for massing was Bart Hess' STRP Mutant series, in which human figures are enveloped in a polymer membrane that simultaneously exposes their form, restrains them, and mutates them. Massing studies aimed to discover a dynamic form wherein the tension between inside and outside is revealed by figural postures as well as surface creases and reliefs. The fluctuating relationship between the 2-D skin and 3-D mass is enhanced by tattooing. The interface of mass-object and drawing-object creates an unexpected overall gestalt. Various digital tools were used for formal generation, including Maya, Grasshopper, and ZBrush.

Tattoo drawings have been studied on their own terms as parallel objects having their own internal rules and figuration. The interface of mass-object and drawing-object created productive feedback in terms of generating surprising overall shapes. The final tattoo captures hard edges as lines and, using the Grasshopper software, generates curves that correspond to the looseness of the surface. The rich effect of the tattoo not only echoes the soft and hard 3-D form but also allows for unusual edge conditions, cusps, and apertures as well as a reflective metallic effect.

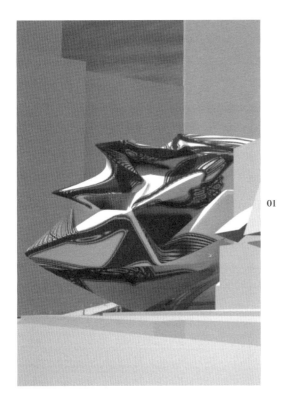

01

(01) The project resulted in a dynamic form wherein the tension between inside and outside is revealed by figural postures as well as surface creases and reliefs.

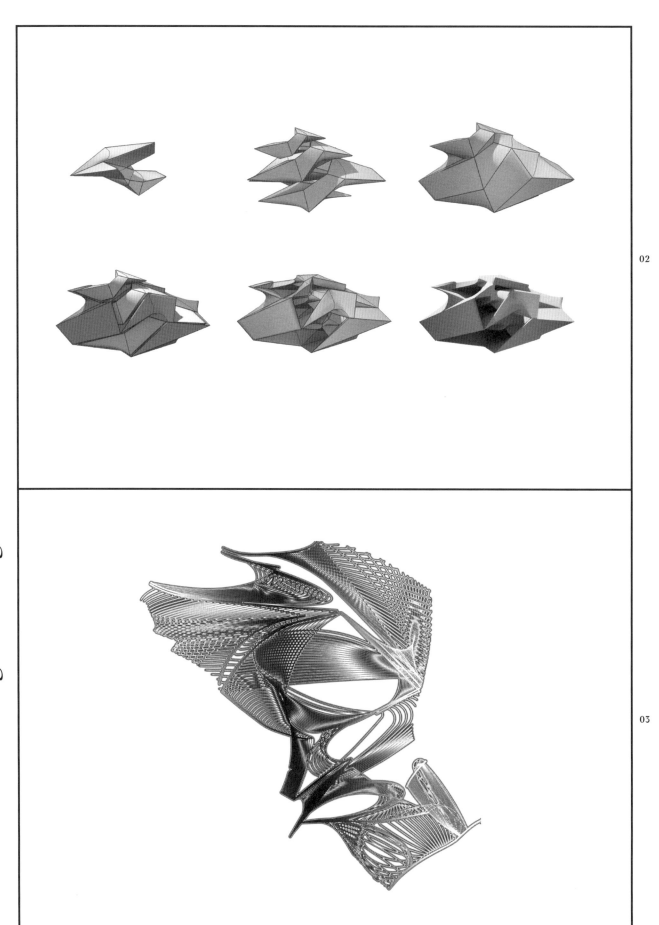

Jing Liu—Figural Feedback

02

03

(02) The inner figure contains three stories of schaulager space; exhibition spaces circulate around it, creating layers of different publicity like a Russian doll. (03) The fluctuating relationship between 2-D skin and 3-D mass is enhanced by tattooing, which has the capacity to either enhance underlying formal features or create artificial depth or flattening.

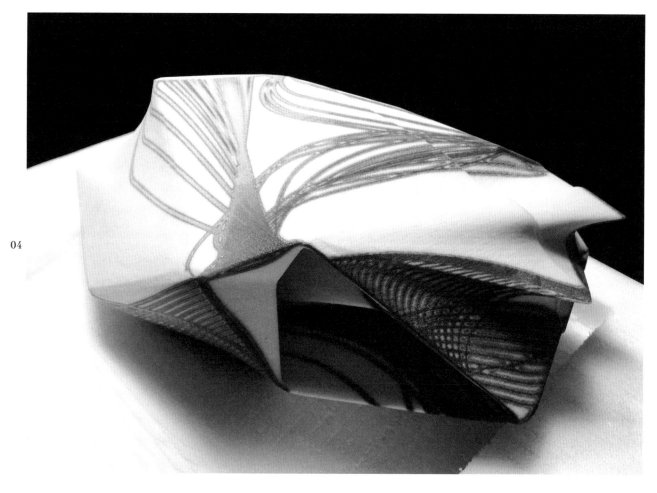

04

05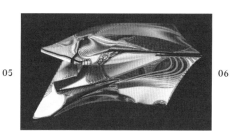

06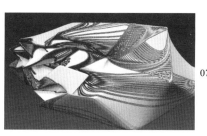

07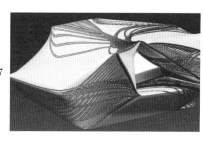

(04) The inner figure becomes starkly visible through a huge aperture that allows the figure to push outside the shell, forming a deep cavity—an ambiguous space mediating inside and outside. (05) The rich effect of the tattoo sometimes exaggerates the soft and hard 3-D form underneath. (06) At times, the tattoo obscures the reading of the underlying volumetric shifts. (07) The tattoo also allows for unusual edge conditions, cusps, and apertures.

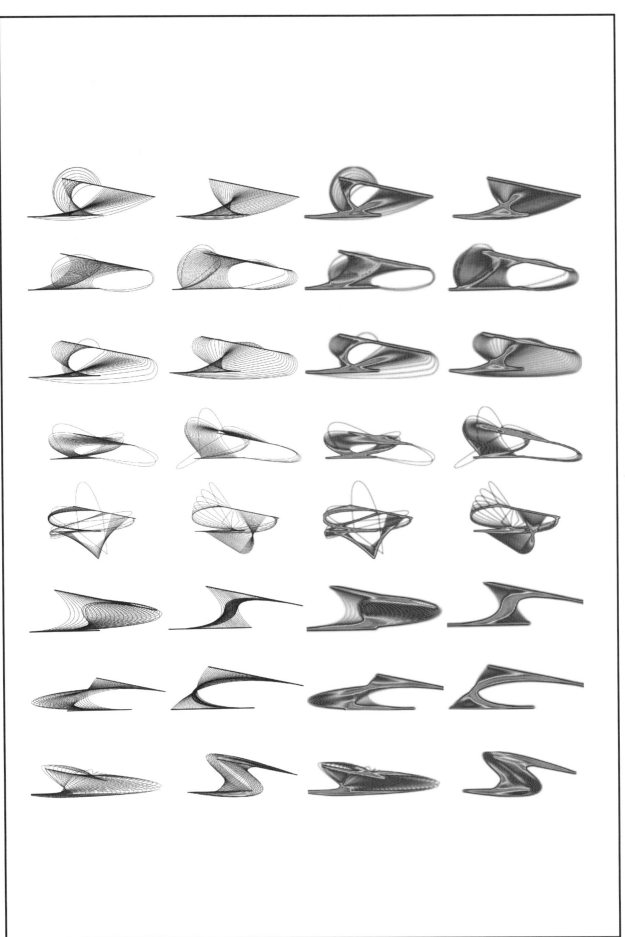

(08) Complex architectural effects were achieved by crossing back
and forth between flat 2-D and extended 3-D formations.

Model 2: Implied Outer Shell

The phrase "implied outer shell" refers to a partial or incomplete enclosure that relies on delaminated and bulging skins to produce space—that is, the container itself becomes spatial; in this way, the project approaches/contemplates/strives for pure poche. Rather than stuffing figures into sacks, figuration emerges from the sack itself. One interesting characteristic of the implied outer shell is that it often produces an indeterminate enclosure so that another system, often glazing, must be used to complete the enclosure. This technique allows for deep views into vast internal spaces in which objects seem to grow out of walls or ceilings. The implied outer shell is a radical form of box-in-a-box architecture. Students who explored this model included Teoman Ayas, Sierra Cobb, and Lauren Page.

Teoman Ayas—Involuted Implied Outer Shell

This project tackles the box-in-a box question though a series of operations applied to a diagrammatically pure organization, as seen in the Beinecke Library, in which the inner box is free-floating. The first operation involves the inner box pushing against the outer skin, as seen in the Tokyo Opera House proposal by Jean Nouvel and Philippe Starck. The next operation involutes the outer skin back around the box, which pushes out against the skin from within. The result is an implied outer shell. This project investigates the spatial and organizational potential of the interstitial space between the box and the skin as well as the methods of generating this space.

In terms of massing, the three main program elements—the schaulager, the gallery, and the auditorium—are represented by three figural objects. Between these figures, an interior cavity is articulated in a softer formal language, contrasting with the sharp lines and corners of the exterior.

On site, the project turns its back toward Grand Avenue and places its outdoor public space back toward Hope Street. The extension covering this outdoor public space parallels the orthogonal, bookend structure of the Disney Concert Hall. The Redcat Theater makes a visual connection though this public space.

The tattoo is applied to key corners of the building and projects over multiple layers of the building skin, breaking down their hierarchy and, practically, puncturing them for lighting.

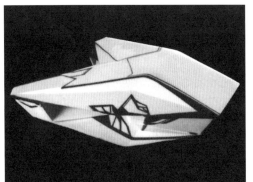

01

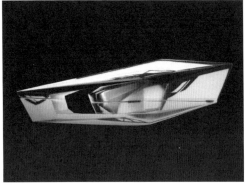

02

(01) This study model develops a language for the tattooed envelope that follows the angular geometry of the overall form. Broad, sweeping strokes connect moments of hyper-intensity that draw visitors toward key moments of interconnectivity. (02) This elevation view demonstrates how all the project components come together to make a whole. The force of the inner boxes pushing against the outer box is expressed as both surface and geometry.

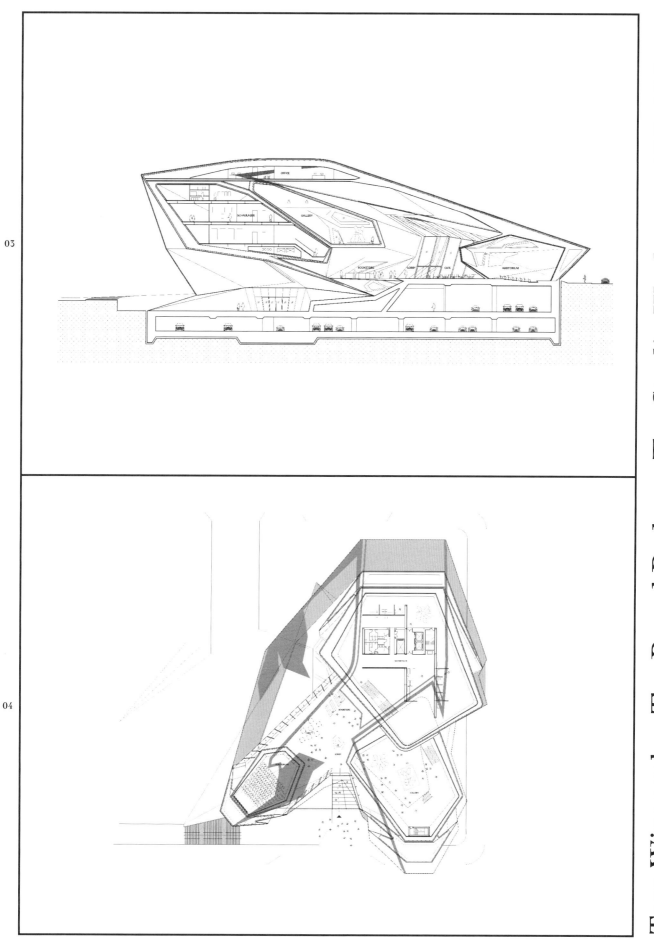

03

04

(03) This is a section through the schaulager, gallery, and auditorium. In fact, these spaces, articulated as independent volumes, are interconnected with the outer skin. This relationship between the inner and outer boxes implies that one is "pushing" on the other, even straining it to the point of causing punctures, edges, and moments of intense articulation. (04) In plan, the three inner boxes are understood as discrete volumes within a larger outer shell. The inner and outer volumes merge at the point of impact and then quickly delaminate into separate surfaces. Between the three inner boxes, a grand interstitial, plaza like space of indeterminate use is formed.

Teoman Ayas—Involuted Implied Outer Shell

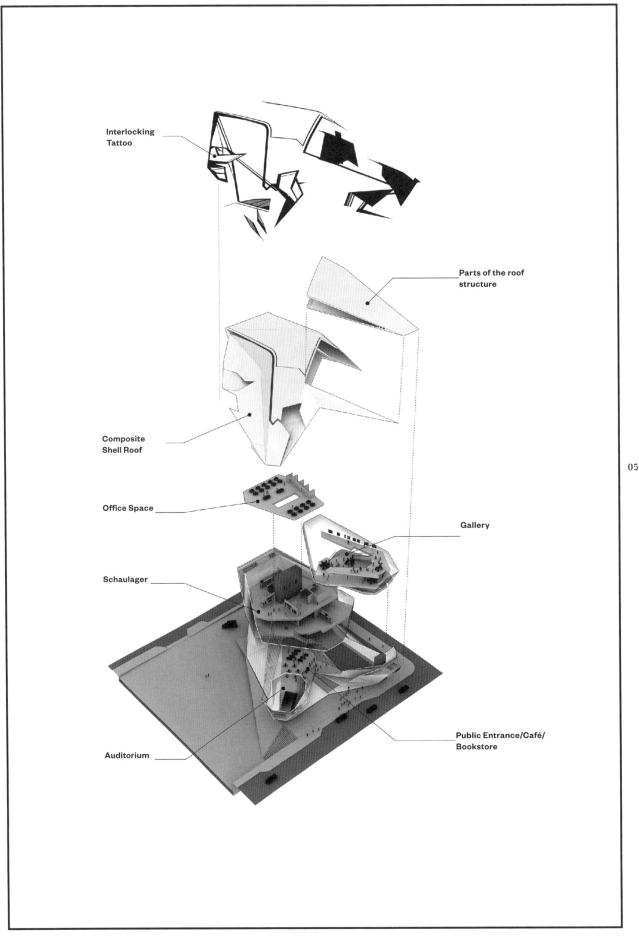

Interlocking Tattoo

Parts of the roof structure

Composite Shell Roof

Office Space

Gallery

Schaulager

Public Entrance/Café/ Bookstore

Auditorium

(05) This drawing illustrates the project's various components as individual systems within a complex, machine like body. In addition to the inner workings of the form, this image includes the outer shell and tattoo as co-generates of the resulting form.

06

07

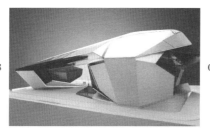

08

09

(06) This southern view illustrates how the outer box is articulated as a complete figure and envelops the interior figures on all sides, including the surface, which meets the ground. (07) With the relative position of the three internal boxes established, this study model explores the relationship between inner and outer volumes and the articulation of the tattooed surface. (08) This view, from the northeast corner of Grand Avenue, shows where the project has turned its back to the street to address the greater amount of activity and transit that already exists along Hope Street. (09) Large glazed apertures define the spaces between the inner boxes. At these moments, the inner and outer shells delaminate, and the two can be seen as a layered proposition, with one nested inside the other.

Sierra Cobb—Flicker

This project explores the idea of the implied outer shell, which is a box-in-a-box wherein the outer shell has collapsed back onto the original figures and, at times, stretches so thin that it disappears. This shell creates interesting moments for interstitial space between outer skin and interior figures. Within this framework, the project employs/hinges upon the "flicker" technique, an architectural effect in which a building appears as a single object and, in the next moment, as multiple objects. The tattoo similarly "flickers" between a 2-D graphic that can flatten space and a 3-D form that can emphasize spatial depth. The vacillation between flatness and depth became the project's main focus, realized by the juxtaposition of transparency and opacity, hard exterior and soft interior forms, and singularity and multiplicity. The site strategy was to isolate the building as a single object, pulling it away from the corners and slightly turning it from the adjacent Disney Concert Hall to face MOCA. Entering the main lobby and exhibition space, the visitor becomes aware that the building is not a single object but two objects coming together. As the visitor progresses further into the space, the objects progressively become more divided. Programmatically, the schaulager and the public exhibition space are sharply differentiated: the former is densely packed within one figure and accessed through the poche, and the latter spills out into open circulation.

The tattoo begins as a demarcation of seams between figures, with moments that imply a trace of where it was before. It then leaves the main geometry and flows past the edges of the outer shell, freeing itself from the three-dimensional form while delineating a new spatial volume.

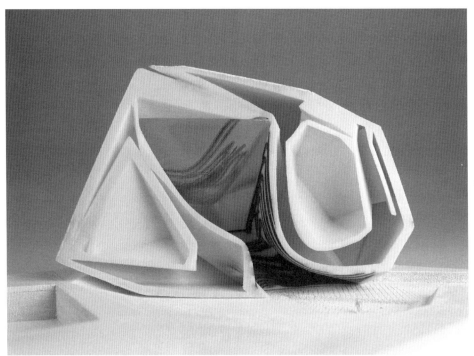

01

(01) View of final sectional model in context, showing the relationship of the building to its base and revealing moments at which the building pulls away from the street, allowing visitors to move under the figures into the exhibition hall beyond.

02

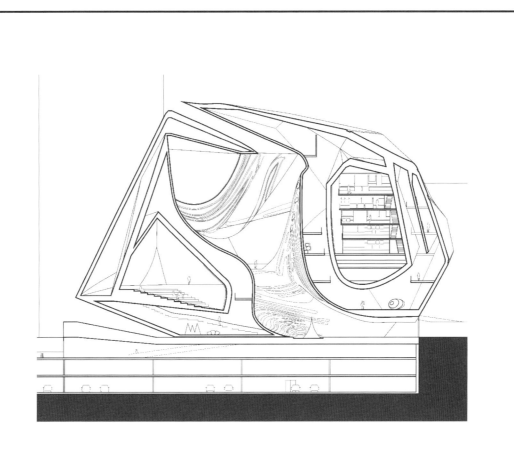

03

(02) The building section describes the primary routes of circulation into the building from the street and from underground. The schaulager is a densely packed, compact chamber for the storage of art. An auditorium is the second dominant figure, nested within the semi-congruent outer skin. The central interstitial space within the building includes fluid program, such as open exhibition space and the lobby. (03) As the graphic morphs across the massing, an oscillation is achieved between perceived flatness and depth.

04

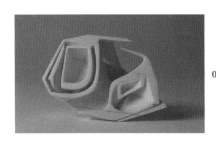

05

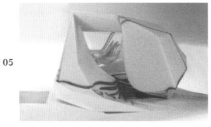

06

07

(04) A close-up view, showing where the building meets the street, demarcated by a deep point of entry. The tattoo is expressive across some surfaces, while others are left blank, distorting the reading of spatial depth as visitors travel deeper into the space. (05) View of a sectional cut through the primary figures and void between. (06) The same view, showing the completed volume with tattoo. (07) An earlier study of the massing morphology.

Lauren Page—Implied Void

The project explores the creation of a spherical envelope as an investigation into the box-within-a-box model. The envelope of the project is loosely fit onto the exterior, revealing internal forms of various orientation and scale, and fit extremely tightly onto the interior, where the forms start to sharply push against the interior skin.

The two internal figures contain a schaulager—a semi-public storage space—and gallery spaces. On the exterior, the schaulager is expressed as a tall figure that creates the rear spine of the overall form and presses against the horizontal figure of the gallery spaces. Within the building, the two figures reach toward each other in a figural dance, creating a dynamic interior sculpture garden. This interstitial zone is legible from the exterior, and suggests a void

extended all the way through the building to the other side. This void is expressed by large glazed apertures on the outer membrane at each end.

The exterior tattoo tracks the edges of the overall form at the two large apertures and bleeds onto the glazing, pushing and pulling the glazing as it travels across it. On the interior, the lines of the tattoo split apart to delineate smaller apertures at various points in the galleries and schaulager where natural light benefits the program. These lines then converge at pressure points where the figures push sharply against the tightly fit interior skin.

Visitors enter the museum through a base plinth, placing them below the figures that dance overhead and frame a view of the interior.

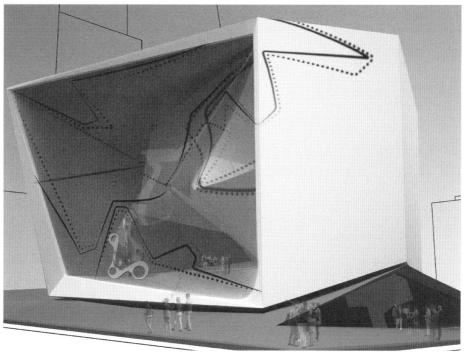

01

(01) Rendering, showing the spine of the Schaulager and the forms through the large aperture

Lauren Page—Implied Void

02

03

(02) View from across Grand Avenue, showing the podium entry and the relationship of the interior forms to the large apertures. (03) The view upon entry to the museum, placing the visitor below the forms of the schaulager and gallery space.

03—Adib Cúre & Carie Penabad, Havana: Housing in the Historic City Center

Interview with Adib Cúre & Carie Penabad by George Knight

Adib Cúre and Carie Penabad discussed their work and their teaching with George Knight principal of Knight Architecture in New Haven and critic at the Yale School of Architecture, prior to the beginning of the Yale studio.

George Knight: How did you meet and decide to start a practice together? Did you always plan to open your own firm?

Carie Penabad: The practice is only one side of the story. Adib and I met at the University of Miami, where our undergraduate teachers, most notably Teofilo Victoria and Roberto Behar, were great inspirations since their practices informed their teaching. It was a fruitful model that initially led us to pursue graduate degrees in urban design at Harvard.

Adib Cúre: While at the GSD, we were taught by dedicated teacher-practitioners Rodolfo Machado, Jorge Silvetti, and Rodolphe el-Khoury, and, upon graduation, we went to work at the office of Machado & Silvetti on a variety of interesting architectural and urban projects, including Dewey Square in Boston and the Getty Villa in Malibu. The office, structured as an atelier, felt like an extension of our academic studio experiences and served as a model for how to build a career that bridges academia and practice.

CP: Simultaneously, we taught at the Boston Architectural College and Northeastern University and pursued the teacher-practitioner model, and then we took full-time positions at the University of Miami. At first it was difficult to move from Boston to Miami, but we felt that developing a practice in a young city that is still trying to develop its identity would provide numerous and varied opportunities for a burgeoning architectural firm.

Your work is wonderfully eclectic, with a broad range of languages and building types. Can you talk a little bit about where you seek inspiration for your work?

AC: For us, inspiration is everywhere. It is in the vernacular and the academic, in the ancient and the contemporary, in the commonplace and the extraordinary. We co-exist comfortably in these two seemingly opposed worlds. Influential for us during our formative years were Vincent Scully's lecture courses at the University of Miami. Scully taught there for more than a decade and passionately spoke to us of the work of the great modern masters, among them Louis Kahn and Robert Venturi, the latter preferring the "both and" to the "either or" and the "black and white" to the "black or white." This all-inclusive sensibility resonated with us.

CP: Our work aspires to create an architecture of place, so we are open to finding beauty in differences and drawn to what makes a place unique. As a result, we are constantly asking ourselves: What is culturally resonant about this place, and how can the work reflect this?

Your work has been lauded by the Congress for New Urbanism (CNU), although in many academic institutions the CNU is perceived as uneven. What do you think about the CNU as a forum for larger issues of urbanism?

AC: New Urbanism's fundamental belief that architecture is a civic act resonates deeply with us. Elizabeth Plater-Zyberk, dean of the University of Miami School of Architecture, has been an influential figure in both our academic and professional lives, and the urban theories of Duany Plater-Zyberk have laid the groundwork for analyzing and thinking about the contemporary city for nearly three decades. Their ideas have now become mainstream, directly influencing both the sustainable-city movement and smart-cities initiatives that guide planning in urban areas throughout the globe.

In the case of Oak Plaza, the project that received the award, we designed a small-scale intervention that had larger repercussions in the development of the Design District, an eighteen-block neighborhood located just north of downtown Miami. When we started working there, it lacked any type of amenity, street life, or public space, and the challenge for us was how to establish a sense of place in an environment that lacked any clear architectural or urban definition. In the end, the first public space produced by the project had a well-defined street and a number of in-fill buildings that strengthened the overall public realm.

Can you describe some of the projects you are excited about in your office?

(01) Oak Plaza, Miami

01

02

(02) MAG Corporate Headquarters, Guatemala, Model

AC: We are currently designing a corporate headquarters for a sugar mill in southern Guatemala. The project has allowed us to confront the challenges of designing a large public building, both with regard to form and construction. Also, the client brief has challenged us to think about the ways in which a building can change the culture of a company and how the design of the physical environment can impact the way in which we communicate.

CP: Interestingly, most of our current work is in Latin America. We have been designing low-income housing models for towns devastated by the recent floods along the northern coast of Colombia as well as projects for new public buildings in two informal settlements just outside the historic city center of Barranquilla, Colombia. Being in Miami provides us with an extraordinary geographic position. We are at the crossroads of North America and South America, and this makes things both exciting and challenging.

You have done a great deal of groundbreaking research into the challenges of informal and developing cities around the world. How have you begun to engage these places, contribute as architects, and learn from them, not only in terms of the specific built environments but also urban growth?

AC: We believe that informal settlements are vernacular expressions of a given people worthy of study. In our view, the informal city has been largely described in social, political, and economic terms, but very little scholarship has been devoted to the study of these cities as works of architecture; and questions of representation—or how to map and record these sites—seems to be missing from the debate. As a result, we have spent the past several years documenting a variety of informal settlements throughout the globe to see first hand how they work. We have attempted to look non-judgmentally at the environment, trying to learn from the place. We are interested in knowing if there are universal themes inherent in the building of these cities as well as what is pertinent to each and distinguishes one from the other.

CP: For instance, we have discovered that Latin American informal settlements develop a clear network of blocks in which buildings always press themselves to the perimeter, clearly defining a street. This is arguably the direct legacy of the Spanish colonial planning traditions, exemplified in countless cities throughout the Americas. However, this is not what we found in the African examples that we studied. Here, it was very difficult to discern any legible block structure. Instead, detached structures were organized around common courts, a possible inheritance of the tribal patterns seen throughout the region.

Why is this important?

We believe there is great wisdom and deeply rooted cultural traditions that establish these urban and architectural patterns; and if architects are going to intervene in these places in a more informed and sensitive way, they need to look and learn before they design.

Interviewing residents also taught us many lessons. For instance, time and time again, we were told that they were capable of building their own houses but desperately needed assistance in the building of the public realm, which necessitates funds from governments or NGOs or both. This may be an area where architects could be of great use. They are also in desperate need of infrastructural connections, be it sewer systems or water supply. The mapping of these sites facilitates the coordination of these complex systems and allows individuals from multiple disciplines to gain an understanding of a place that has existed literally "off the map" or that appears daunting and incomprehensible from an aerial perspective.

Do you foresee not only research but also a professional approach to such projects? What patterns within the profession of architecture do you see responding to this groundswell for more informed city planning?

CP: The reality is that this is an ever-growing urban phenomenon. According to the World Bank, since World War II, global population has increased to 5.5 billion from 2 billion, and nearly all this growth has taken place in the developing world where the urban population has grown from 300 million to approximately 1.7 billion today. Most of these urban dwellers live in informal cities. Given this reality, it is vital that we deepen our understanding of this urban phenomenon and its multiple manifestations. We have seen two models for working within the informal city throughout our travels. There are grassroots efforts and organizations rising out of the informal settlements that architects can engage with. We have seen an alternate model work successfully in Colombia, where the government has initiated public design competitions, to which young architects can submit their work. Projects have focused on the design of the public realm and infrastructural projects that, in many instances, have transformed these places. We imagine that, in the future, architects working within these worlds will need

(03) MDO, Miami, Rear Elevation

to move easily between the micro and the macro.

AC: We are working in an interdisciplinary way with sociologists, anthropologists, lawyers, economists, and community activists. We believe that a collaborative model yields more informed fruitful design solutions. To this end, we recently organized an international symposium at the University of Miami titled "Dialogues with the Informal City: Latin America and the Caribbean." The event was organized around four cross-cutting themes that were capable of engaging a wide range of issues and differing disciplinary perspectives.

Earlier, Carie, you talked about drawing the urban settlements to make them real, which is paradoxical: that drawing the real thing makes the real thing more real. Can you elaborate on your teaching, and what you see as the role of drawing for architects?

CP: Drawing these cities makes them visible and, thus, allows us to see them anew.

Today, there is a general preoccupation, and even angst, in the profession regarding drawing. The advent of the computer has displaced long-established drawing traditions that have put into question not only what we draw but how we draw it. For me, it is less interesting when the discourse focuses on medium and more

so when it dwells on thinking about how one acquires knowledge of the workings of the visual world in order to design within it. This is the timeless pursuit of the architect and one that remains relevant when the latest computer program has become obsolete. In our own work, we explore a variety of digital and hand drawings. Yet, we still find the sketch the most immediate and profound way to develop an architectural idea. For us, the act of sketching is multi-sensorial and involves the development of muscular memory ignited by the physical act of placing marks on a sheet of paper and the recollection of that experience as a visual imprint in the mind. We believe in drawing as a way of gaining architectural knowledge, and we are interested in recording the more phenomenological aspects of place associated with light and color—and perhaps this is what informs our preoccupation with creating works of architecture that are sensitized to the particulars of place and time. I believe that, in the end, the debate about drawing is really a debate about architecture or what you believe architecture should be. One informs the other.

Could you tell us about your spring studio at Yale?

AC: We will be focusing on a study of Havana's historic city center, which is a particularly poignant example for

us because it is a place where the formal and informal physically overlap and coexist. Today, much of the fabric is occupied by individuals living in sub standard conditions. We believe there needs to be an effort to not only stop the decline through the preservation and retrofit of existing structures but also to develop new housing models capable of addressing the needs of a contemporary society.

Could you tell us about your current work?

CP: The office is currently working on a number of projects of varying size and scope including a master plan for an educational campus, the corporate headquarters for a sugar mill and residential designs ranging from interiors to courtyard housing typologies for new urban developments. The firm is also collaborating with non-for-profit agencies to develop new classroom prototypes for educational buildings to be used in impoverished rural areas of Guatemala. The first of these prototypes is currently under construction and will be completed at the end of the year. Beyond the architectural/urban commissions, the firm has been designing a number of custom furnishings and hardware and is developing a line of concrete floor tiles to be released in 2016.

Havana: Housing in the Historic City Center

"The grid [of Havana] appears dictated by the primordial, tropical necessity of playing hide-and-seek with the sun, laughing at its surfaces, exposing shaded areas, and fleeing from the torrid announcements of twilight."
— Carpentier, Alejo. *Las Ciudad de las Columnas*. Pozuelo de Alarcón, Espasa Calpe, 2004

Project description

The degradation and neglect of the city center is a pressing urban and architectural problem facing many cities in Latin America. Considering the relevance of historic centers as providers of character for a given city and as the origin of the identity of that particular city, there should be an effort not only to stop the existing decline through the preservation of existing structures but also to improve the living conditions through the incorporation of new housing models that are capable of addressing the needs of contemporary society. Nowhere is this challenge more poignant than in Havana, Cuba. Havana is one of the richest and most eclectic urban environments in the Americas, but it is largely crumbling. The city's urban development has been dramatically different than other nearby Spanish colonial cities, such as San Juan or Cartagena de Indias. These sites have experienced the more typical cycles of decline and preservation associated with free-market economies, including the mass exodus to the suburbs after World War II and the recent restoration efforts to transform the historic center into a profitable tourist destination.

Such planning is not the case in Havana, as the political and economic context prevented this from occurring. As a result, the historic center was never abandoned, but, rather, the city grew from within. Today, much of the colonial fabric, as well as the palatial residences of the Republican era, is occupied by individuals living in substandard conditions. How can we introduce new housing typologies that are capable of addressing the city's contemporary needs? And how can we build the new city as both a reflection of our times as well as a coherent addition to Havana's rich architectural legacy?

To this end, the semester focused on the design of new housing projects for Central Havana, the city's densest and most deteriorated sector and, in our view, the one in greatest need of design intervention. Central Havana has an extraordinary building stock, but it is veiled by decades of deterioration; moreover, the sector lacks the allure of the adjacent colonial city and El Vedado, districts that have historically housed the city's elite and, as such, contain larger, more significant building footprints. Conversely, Central Havana has always been the working-class district, developed with smaller, more modest parcels and limited open space. These realities, compounded by the fact that it lies outside the boundaries of UNESCO's World Heritage Site designation, make it far more vulnerable with regard to future land speculation.

01

(01) Location map, showing Central Havana in the context of greater Havana. Old Havana is located directly east, and Vedado is to the west. The project sites are strung along Galiano Street, which runs north-south through eastern Central Havana.

(02) Panorama of Central Havana. (03/04) Street in Old Havana.

Havana: A Brief Urban History

The urban historical geography of Havana bears the imprint of a city originally inhabited by native Indians, designed and ruled by the Spanish, modernized by the United States, and, ultimately, governed by a centrally planned, Cuban, communist government.

Little remains of the Guanajatabeyes, Siboneyes, and Taino tribes that originally inhabited the island. The indigenous population clustered in villages, called bateyes, typically situated on the coast near the mouth of a river or in the hills rising above swampy areas. Individual houses, called bohios, were built of straw and palm-tree leaves, typically raised from the ground with steep, ventilated roofs. The term is still used today to describe the small rural huts of the Cuban countryside.

The arrival of the Spanish, with their guns and diseases, eradicated most of the native population. Between 1500 and 1515, an expedition of about three hundred Spaniards, led by explorer and governor Diego Velázquez de Cuéllar, landed on the island in search of mineral wealth. They established seven military outposts, called villas, including Baracoa (1512), Bayamo (1513), Trinidad (1514), Sancti Spiritus (1514), San Cristobal de la Habana (founded in 1514 on the southern coast and then, in 1519, on the northern coast), Santiago de Cuba (1515), and Puerto Principe (founded in 1514, but moved inland to Camaguey in 1528). The founding of these seven settlements determined the urbanization of the island.

San Cristobal de la Habana was first located on the Broa Inlet, just off the Gulf of Batabano, along Cuba's southern coast. The undesirable environment and the shallow port forced the settlement to be relocated; and, in 1519, the villa of Havana moved to the northeastern shore of the island. The precise site of this settlement is unknown; however, it is thought to have been located at the mouth of the Almendares River. Here, the villa had direct access to fresh water but was vulnerable to rising seas and lacked a sheltered harbor. As a result, the villa was moved one last time, to the western side of a large deepwater bay, just a few kilometers east (Scarpaci, Segre, Coyula, 11-12).

Havana slowly developed along the edge of the bay through a series of plazas that pressed close to the water's edge. A network of *calzadas*, or narrow streets, was developed perpendicular to the waterfront, terminating in the fortifications that later encircled the city to the west. The city's geographic location made it a critical trans-shipment point in the commerce between the Old World and the New. Havana's harbor was a safe haven, capable of supplying Spanish galleons with essential provisions for the treacherous, nearly 6,000-mile journey between Seville, Spain, and Veracruz, Mexico. Quickly realizing the strategic location of the city, the Spaniards moved the governorship from Santiago de Cuba to Havana, making it the most important villa on the island.

Initially, as Bartolomé de las Casas suggests in his chronicle *Historia de las Indias*, the Spaniards adopted indigenous housing typologies that were constructed of wood and thatch, easily erected, and well-suited to the local climate. However, this fragile wooden architecture was prone to fires, and the abundant use of palm thatch in its construction depleted local farmers from palmiche,

a food staple for their animals. As a result, the Spaniards quickly shifted to an architecture of stone and masonry, and directly impacted both the typology and architectural language of Havana's domestic architecture, most notably the adoption and proliferation of the Spanish patio house.

For the remainder of the sixteenth and much of the seventeenth centuries, Spanish builders and engineers were occupied with the construction of important infrastructural projects, including an extensive network of fortifications as well as numerous public buildings: the Convent of Saint Francis, the Aduana, and the Saint Felipe and Santiago Hospital, among others. Few examples of

05

06

07

(05) Studio on the Malecon. (06) On the roof of Vittorio Garatti's School of Ballet. (07) In-fill patterns typical of Havana.

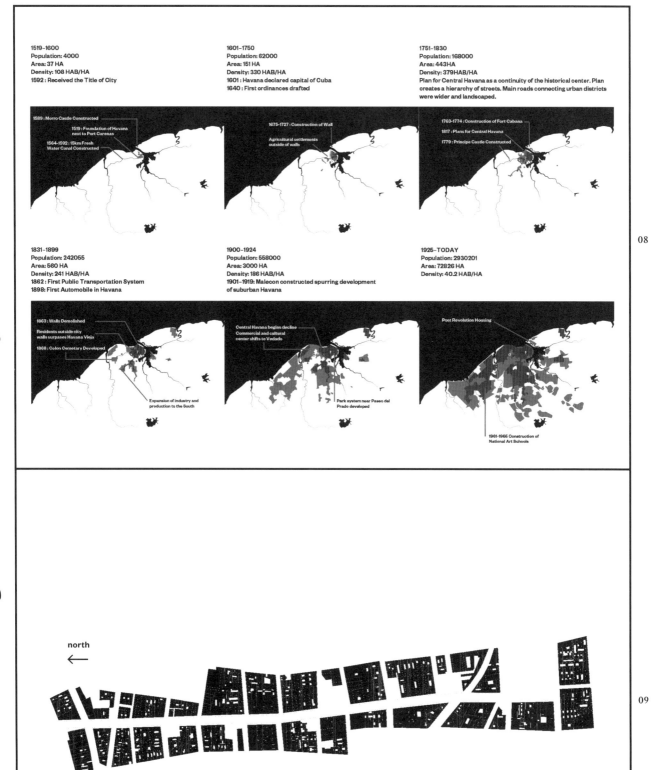

1519–1600
Population: 4000
Area: 37 HA
Density: 108 HAB/HA
1592 : Received the Title of City

1601–1750
Population: 62000
Area: 151 HA
Density: 330 HAB/HA
1601 : Havana declared capital of Cuba
1640 : First ordinances drafted

1751–1830
Population: 168000
Area: 443HA
Density: 379HAB/HA

Plan for Central Havana as a continuity of the historical center. Plan creates a hierarchy of streets. Main roads connecting urban districts were wider and landscaped.

1831–1899
Population: 242055
Area: 560 HA
Density: 241 HAB/HA
1862 : First Public Transportation System
1898: First Automobile in Havana

1900–1924
Population: 558000
Area: 3000 HA
Density: 186 HAB/HA
1901–1919: Malecon constructed spurring development of suburban Havana

1925–TODAY
Population: 2930201
Area: 72826 HA
Density: 40.2 HAB/HA

north

(08) Diagrams charting the growth of Havana from the early sixteenth century to the present. Central Havana was developed after the city outgrew its original walled boundary. (09) Figure-ground analysis of Galiano Street, revealing the fine urban grain of Central Havana. The potential sites consist of several of the many vacant lots lining this major street.

10

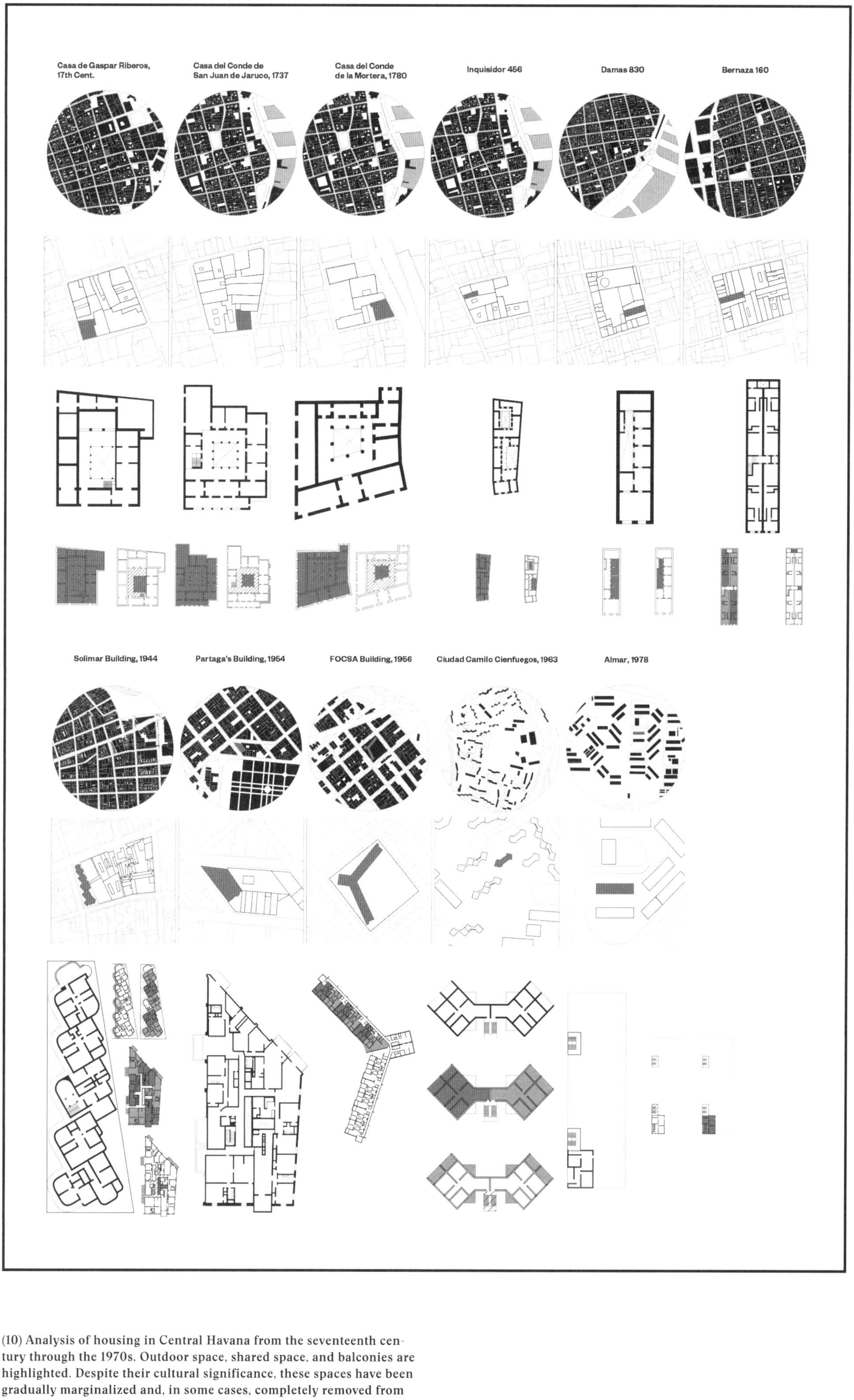

Casa de Gaspar Riberos, 17th Cent.

Casa del Conde de San Juan de Jaruco, 1737

Casa del Conde de la Mortera, 1780

Inquisidor 456

Damas 830

Bernaza 160

Solimar Building, 1944

Partaga's Building, 1954

FOCSA Building, 1956

Ciudad Camilo Cienfuegos, 1963

Almar, 1978

(10) Analysis of housing in Central Havana from the seventeenth century through the 1970s. Outdoor space, shared space, and balconies are highlighted. Despite their cultural significance, these spaces have been gradually marginalized and, in some cases, completely removed from housing types in Havana.

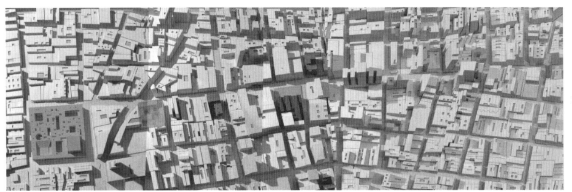

(12) The large studio site model shows Galiano Street and its surrounding blocks as seen from above. The Malecon and the coast are shown on the right of the model. The student proposals have been highlighted.

domestic architecture survive from this period (Casa de Paula, Casa de Obispo 117 and 119). These early residences were one- or two-story stone-and-rubble structures with tiled roofs and a central rectangular patio, which allowed for greater light and ventilation. In the two-story version, the first floor was typically used for commerce and storage, while the upper level served as the family residence; on this floor, the most important public rooms (living room, dining room, kitchen) lined the street, and the bedrooms were displaced toward the rear of the lot, alongside the patio. In time, the patio house became larger, more stylized, and reflected the changing architectural styles of the day; however, the constituent elements of the type remained remarkably consistent for more than four centuries.

The development of Modern architecture in Cuba occurred roughly between 1925 and 1965. This period was the culmination of dramatic political and social changes that took place at the end of the nineteenth century, most importantly the brief American occupation of the island following the Spanish American War. Local architects adopted the tenants of the International Style while searching to adapt its principles to the particulars of the Cuban context. Central Havana boasts the leading examples of this period's architectural works, El Vedado and Miramar, the nineteenth- and twentieth-century expansions of the fortified colonial city.

In 1955, the government established a National Planning Board, charged with the task of regulating the urban expansion of the city. Soon after its founding, the board hired the firm of Town Planning Associates, directed by Josep Lluis Sert and Paul Lester Wiener, to draw a regulatory plan for Havana. The plan established regulations for the protection of small business, height restrictions, an increase in recreational and green open spaces, and more. However, had the plan been implemented, it would have done away with many treasured parts of the city, sacrificing them on the altar of an imposed modernity (Eduardo Luis Rodriguez, *The Havana Guide: Modern Architecture*, 1925–1965). In the end, Cuba's so-called Modern Movement brought a flourishing of new architectural and urban design ideas, but it also aggravated a range of social and urban problems, including the neglect of low-cost housing, unfettered land speculation, and the visual assault of aggressive high-rise buildings that blatantly disregarded the existing urban environment.

Initially, the victory of the Cuban revolution, in 1959, did not provoke a sudden break in the evolution of modern architecture on the island. Notable works continued to be developed, despite the shifting social and philosophical context. The project that best exemplifies this period is the unfinished complex of the new National Art Schools, started in 1961 and continued until 1965, by Ricardo Porro, Vittorio Garatti, and Roberto Gottardi. However, the new political regime slowly began to exert its influence on all aspects of society, prompting the exile of Cuba's leading Modernist architects and, in 1965, the closure of the College of Architects. The regime shifted its focus to the production of low-cost housing, modeled largely on post-World War II Soviet housing projects. These developments, located on the outskirts of Cuba's leading cities, produced bleak urban landscapes that displaced the populace from the rich urban housing tradition, which had characterized the island for nearly five centuries. In recent decades, the exodus to the suburbs has been reversed with rural populations returning to urban centers (particularly Havana) in a desperate search for a better way of life. The once majestic historic city is now a continuous vertical slum. The crumbling infrastructure, with its lack of running water and adequate sewage, has produced nearly intolerable conditions that are the norm versus the exception of life in Havana today. The current government has begun to invest in the restoration of existing buildings (mainly public buildings and hotels) to continue to lure tourists to the island. Yet for Havana to have any real and viable future beyond a fabricated tourist destination, the preservation and construction of the urban fabric must rise to the foreground as a vital urban and architectural project.

The Project Site: Central Havana, Galiano Street

Central Havana is located just west of the original fortified city. The district is bordered by the Malecon, Havana's waterfront promenade, to the north; Old Havana to the east, and the garden-city El Vedado to the west. It is the most densely populated and architecturally diverse district in the city. The current population is estimated at

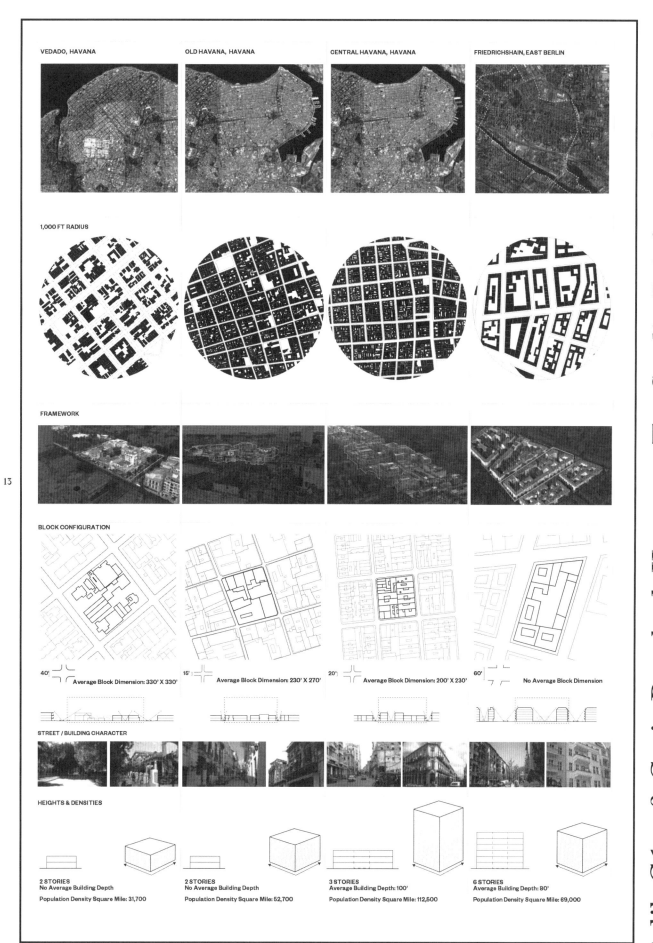

VEDADO, HAVANA — OLD HAVANA, HAVANA — CENTRAL HAVANA, HAVANA — FRIEDRICHSHAIN, EAST BERLIN

1,000 FT RADIUS

FRAMEWORK

13

BLOCK CONFIGURATION

40' — Average Block Dimension: 330' X 330'
15' — Average Block Dimension: 230' X 270'
20' — Average Block Dimension: 200' X 230'
60' — No Average Block Dimension

STREET / BUILDING CHARACTER

HEIGHTS & DENSITIES

2 STORIES
No Average Building Depth
Population Density Square Mile: 31,700

2 STORIES
No Average Building Depth
Population Density Square Mile: 52,700

3 STORIES
Average Building Depth: 100'
Population Density Square Mile: 112,500

6 STORIES
Average Building Depth: 80'
Population Density Square Mile: 69,000

(13) Density analysis of districts in cities around the globe in comparison with Central Havana. Selected locations are Vedado, Havana; Old Havana; Friedrichshain, Berlin; Eixample, Barcelona; Soho, New York; Aoyama, Tokyo; and the Spanish Quarter, Naples.

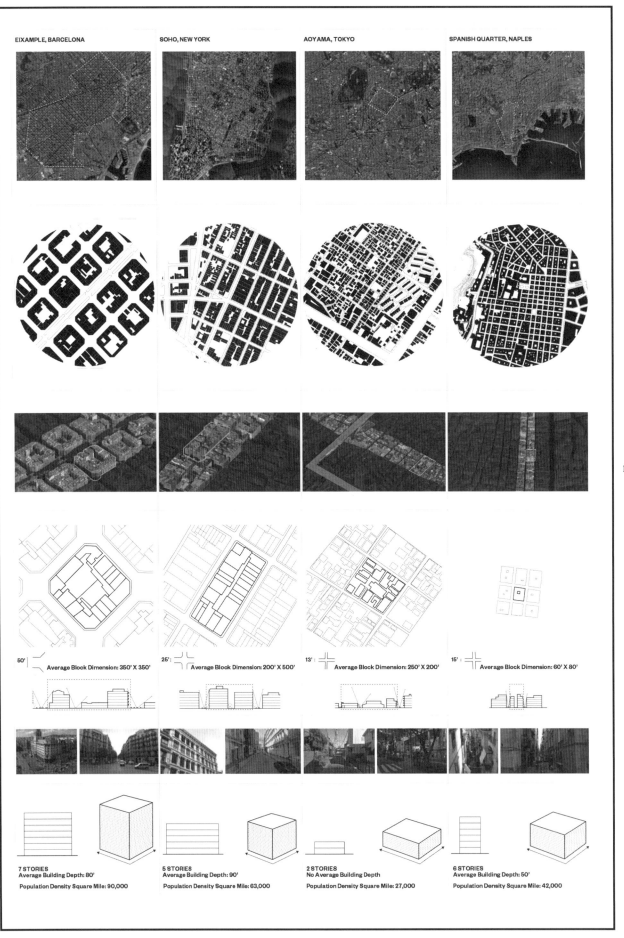

Havana: Housing in the Historic City Center

EIXAMPLE, BARCELONA   SOHO, NEW YORK   AOYAMA, TOKYO   SPANISH QUARTER, NAPLES

50' Average Block Dimension: 350' X 350'

25' Average Block Dimension: 200' X 500'

13' Average Block Dimension: 250' X 200'

15' Average Block Dimension: 60' X 80'

7 STORIES
Average Building Depth: 80'
Population Density Square Mile: 90,000

5 STORIES
Average Building Depth: 90'
Population Density Square Mile: 63,000

2 STORIES
No Average Building Depth
Population Density Square Mile: 27,000

6 STORIES
Average Building Depth: 50'
Population Density Square Mile: 42,000

14

(14) Density analysis of districts in cities around the globe in compar-
ison with Central Havana. Selected locations are Vedado, Havana; Old
Havana; Friedrichshain, Berlin; Eixample, Barcelona; SoHo, New York;
Aoyama, Tokyo; and the Spanish Quarter, Naples.

154,000, most of whom live in highly precarious housing stock in unsanitary conditions. Dating to the early 1700s, Central Havana was the first urban extension of the original fortified city. Originally, the site comprised agricultural lands that were used to supply the Spanish fleet with provisions for its journey across the Atlantic. A small church (1716), devoted to the Virgin of Guadalupe and located at the intersection of Monte and Aguila streets, marks the center of the first neighborhood. The relocation, in 1734, of the Royal Arsenal to the south and, in 1772, the creation of the Alameda de Extramuros, or the "Off the Walls Promenade," contributed to the expansion of the district. In 1817, the *plan de ensanche*, or "regulating plan," the first of its kind in Havana, guided the growth of the city beyond the recently demolished fortification walls; in an orderly manner, the plan capitalized on the exiting layout of original roads, which connected the walled city with the countryside. The plan further established a hierarchy of streets in which the *calzadas*, or "main arteries," would become the most distinctive feature of Havana's new streetscape, standing in sharp contrast to the character of Old Havana's streets. The original calzadas turned into commercial axes that were later sheltered with Neo-Classical porticoes and arcades, an emblematic architectural element associated with the city (Coyula, 29).

Methodology

The work of the semester was divided into two parts: analysis and architectural project. The semester began with a comprehensive urban mapping and typological analysis that allowed the studio to understand the richly layered history of the contemporary city and the many transformations that have led to its present form. Students were asked to carefully study the current urban conditions as well as the relationships between the urban pattern and its correspondent architecture, focusing on the most culturally and tectonically resonant elements of the city's composition. Housing projects were then considered for a variety of sites along Galiano Street, one of Central Havana's principal commercial thoroughfares. Galiano served as a case study to examine common conditions associated with the current housing crisis including vacant lots, in which structures have recently crumbled due to decades of neglect, and historic buildings in an advanced state of decay transformed into solares or barbacoas—that is, substandard housing developments. The final architectural projects were viewed as urban-architectural acupuncture, a concentrated and focused effort to insert a new housing stock amid the deteriorated infrastructure of the existing fabric. In the development of the projects, the studio was interested in developing strategies that could be repeated throughout the district as viable models for the future integration of the built city.

All projects were developed as mixed use, with commercial or public functions at grade and apartments on the upper stories. The size, configuration, and density of the housing units was analyzed and tested in accordance to universal housing standards as well as the contemporary code for Central Havana, legislation that defines the current production of new housing for the city today.

Bibliography

Barclay, Juliet. *Havana: Portrait of a City*. London: Cassel, 1993.

Carpentier, Alejo. *La Ciudad de las Columnas*. Barcelona: Bruguera, S.A., 1982.

Drakakis-Smith, David. *Third World Cities*. 2nd ed. London: Routledge, 2000.

Duany, Andrés. 'The Future of Havana.' In *One World: Shared Cultural Influences in the Architecture of the Americas*. Miami: Association of Collegiate Schools of Architecture, University of Miami: 35-36, 1997.

Hardoy, Jorge E. 'The Building of Latin American Cities', in A.Gilbert; J.Hardoy; R. Ramirez (ed). *Urbanization in Contemporary Latin America, Critical Approaches to the Analysis of Urban Issues*. New York, John Wiley & Sons: 19-33, 1982.

Hernandez, Felipe; Kellett, Peter; Allen, Lea K. *Rethinking the Informal City: Critical Perspectives From Latin America*. New York: Berghahn Books, 2010.

Lowder, Stella. *The Geography of Third World Cities*. Totowa, New Jersey: Barnes & Noble Books, 1986.

Rigau, J., and N. Stout. *Havana*. New York: Rizzoli, 1994.

Rodriguez, Eduardo Luis. *The Havana Guide: Modern Architecture, 1925-1965*. New York: Princeton Architectural Press, 2000.

Scarpaci, Joseph L.; Segre, Roberto; Coyula, Mario *Havana: Two Faces of the Antillean Metropolis*. Chapel Hill and London: The University of North Carolina Press, 2002.

Suchlicki, Jaime. *Cuba: From Columbus to Castro and Beyond*. Washington: Brassey's, Inc., 1997.

Tung, Anthony M. *Preserving the World's Greatest Cities: The Destruction and Renewal of the Historic Metropolis*. New York: Random House, Inc., 2001.

14

(14) Revolution era apartment block

Studio Work

Galiano: Tacon District

The Tacon District is one of the largest sectors defining the south-eastern edge of Galiano Street. Located immediately adjacent to Havana's Chinatown, it contains a patchwork of eclectic buildings of varying scales. The district was the site of the historic Tacon Market, since demolished and now a vacant parcel. Projects in this district explored a variety of themes, including the reintroduction of a contemporary market for the city.

Christina Argyros—Bazaar Urbanism

Havana is defined by the critical density at its center:
The narrow streets are limited by buildings that con-
ceal their interior patios and communal spaces. One
could argue that the activity of life in the city happens
on the street, leaving interior patios in a state of neglect
and decay. Rather than providing points of urban
interaction within the city fabric, such spaces end up
neglected as empty voids. This project occupies an
entire empty block and exhibits the morphological richness of the existing city through alterations between
dense volumes and empty spaces as well as a func-
tional gradient between public and private use, thus
creating an entire new neighborhood for the city.

Markets historically have been central community
nodes, spaces that naturally emerge from within the
city fabric and entail urban congestion. Considering the
numerous empty voids within the city of Havana, this
project attempts to rethink the function of these voids
as centers of activity by inserting within them the informality of the market while bringing the urban street
back into the housing block, thus creating small-scale
plazas within the larger city. What matters most is that
which happens in the urban voids, those places in the
city that leave room for the unanticipated.

01

(01) Preliminary study models, showing progress from early concepts
to the final proposal. Early investigations focused on bringing the circulation of the city into the block itself. A variety of scales were tested
for open spaces within the block.

02

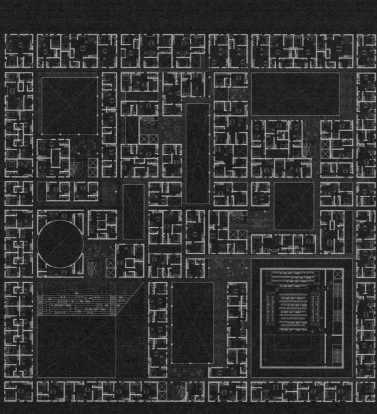

03

(02) An aerial view of the final proposal model. Multiple specialized functions are present in the design, including a terraced sports court, open patios, and a large theater housed in the tall volume. (03) The third floor plan shows the aggregation of housing units as neighborhoods centered on public open spaces.

Christina Argyros—Bazaar Urbanism

(04) The proposal shown in the larger studio site model. The fine urban grain of Central Havana continues into the project through a variety of carefully scaled open spaces.

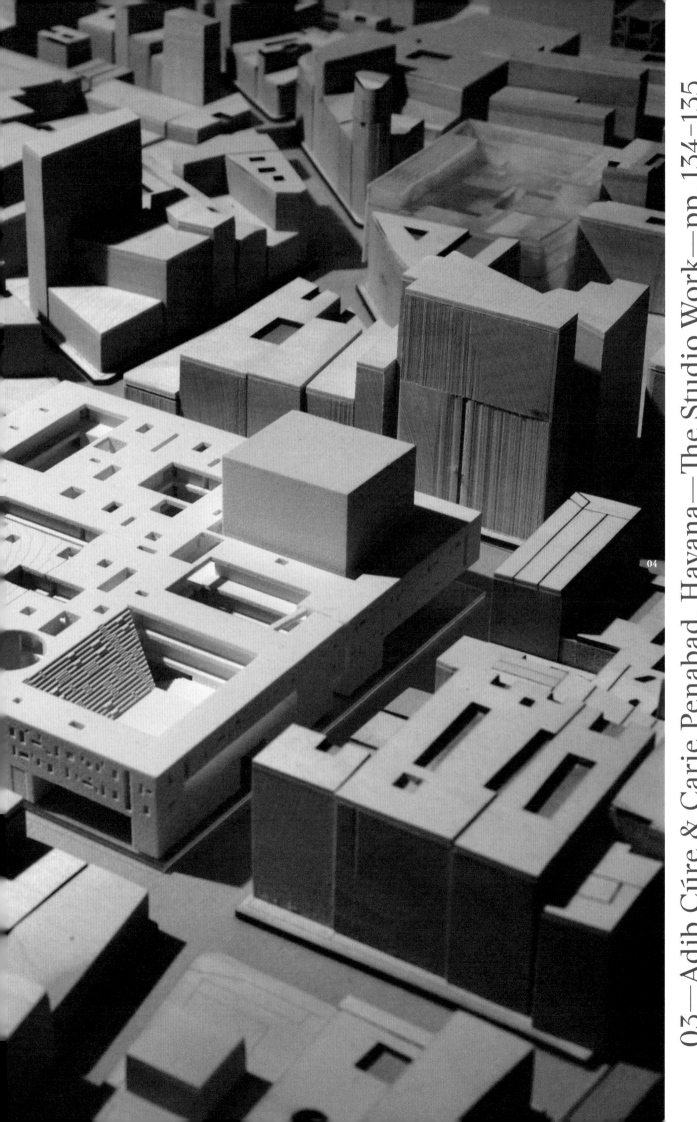

04

Antonia Devine—Urban Agripuncture

This proposal for housing in Central Havana is based upon the idea of introducing urban agriculture—or urban farms, known as organoponicos—with courtyard-centric housing units. The result is a live-work model in which residents can grow food in their housing courtyards for either consumption or sale. Cuba has a complex food history with food that, most recently, includes many years of near starvation due to the abeyance of the agricultural industry. During this time, Cubans have begun growing produce in abandoned lots on the periphery of Havana. Despite this capacity for agricultural production, the transportation network for this produce lacks systemization and remains undeveloped; in fact, this food does not manage to make its way into the city. Thus, this project proposes the urban farm and its benefits: easy, direct community access to the produce as well as community-generated jobs.

Both of these goals can be accomplished by introducing organoponicos into the private housing courtyards. The urban farm consists of low concrete beds filled with composted sugar waste and serviced by drip irrigation. Beginning with the existing model of the Cuban courtyard, this typology is stacked and divided to create communal areas with differing amounts of sunshine to accommodate a variety of crops as well as offer afternoon shade for socializing. All of these exterior spaces are connected by a central, processional, open-air stair. The apartments range from one- to three-bedroom units that have narrow floor plates for cross-ventilation and natural light and either private patios or kitchens that open onto the central courtyard. While every resident has access to the courtyards, the ground floor houses a restaurant, shops, and primary and secondary lobbies for residents.

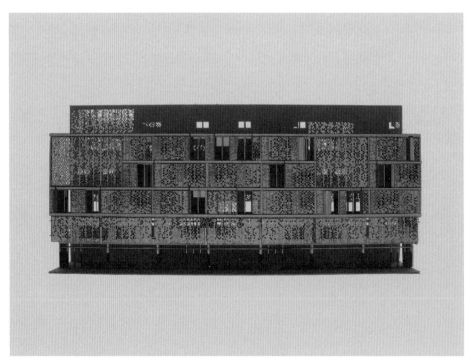

01

(01) A preliminary model of the Galiano Street facade screen shows the perforations and shadow effects they create. Housing units have large, operable windows, while double-height public courtyards show through to the facade on the fourth and fifth floors.

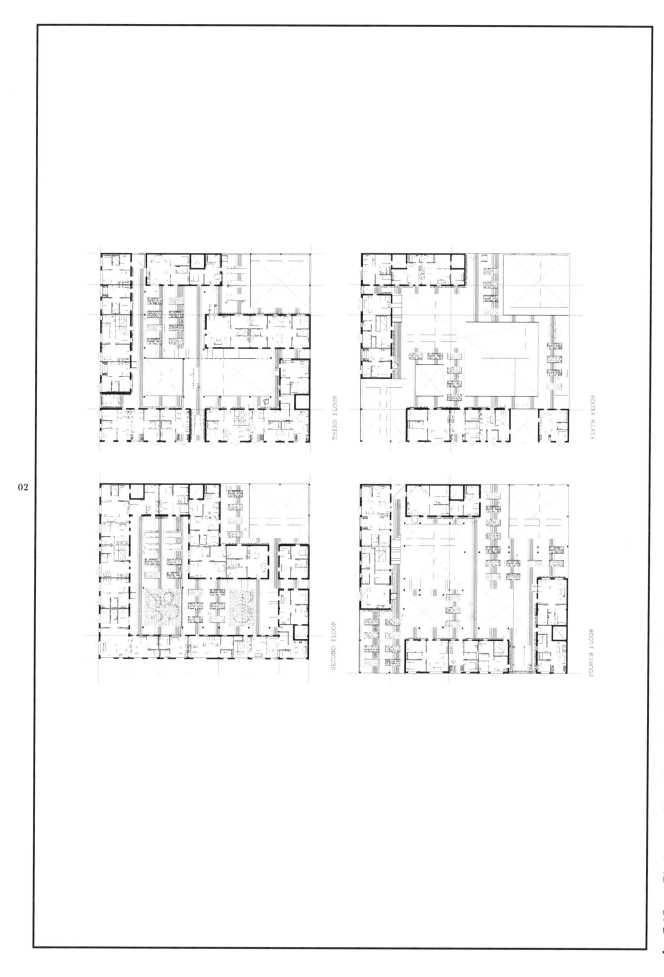

02

THIRD FLOOR

FIFTH FLOOR

SECOND FLOOR

FOURTH FLOOR

(02) Upper-level floor plans. Housing units are gathered around public
courtyards, where the organoponicos are located. These courtyards
enlarge on the higher floors to allow light and air into the lower levels.

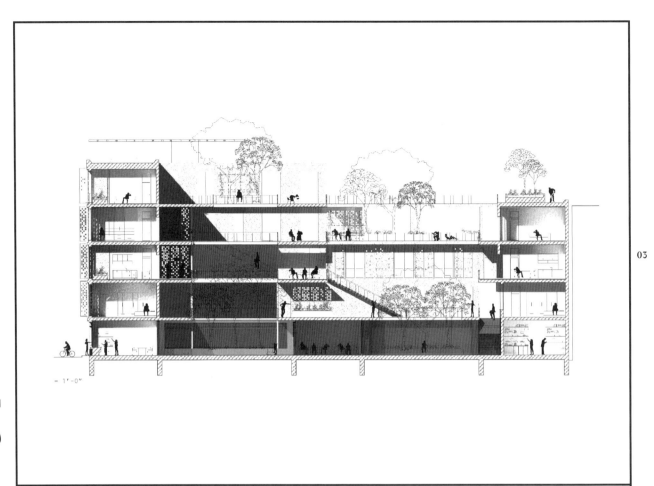

(03) The longitudinal section through the proposal shows the public courtyards and their organoponicos located in the center of the lot. A large public stair rises through the center of these courtyards to join together the multiple levels. The housing units line the edges of the lot. (04) Elevation, showing the Galiano Street facade. The upper floors are shielded from the western sun by a perforated screen, which overhangs the sidewalk to offer a variation on the continuous arcade seen along the street. At the ground level, shops and the restaurant front onto Galiano.

Katharine Storr—Havana Dom-ino

This project attempts to solve the infrastructural limitations on housing in Central Havana by tapping into the existing culture of self-built housing and creating a framework within which residents can shape their own space. Preliminary research focused on the average amount of square footage in which residents of different countries around the globe are used to living. Cuban standards are far below those in most other Western countries, with the footprint of an average three-adult, one-child household in Central Havana being roughly equal to the average space occupied per person in Spain or the United Kingdom.

Drawing primary inspiration from Le Corbusier's Dom-ino framework concept, the building initially consists only of structure, building systems, circulation, communal space, retail, and a pocket park at the rear of the site. As families move in, they can appropriate space within the framework and build their own homes by connecting to the existing services provided within the cores. The roof of the building is oriented so that it slopes inward to catch the rain, which is stored on site for later use by the residents. The robust concrete structure is designed to withstand the continual reconfiguration of housing units that would be typical in the building. The rhythm of the columns suggests a standard housing unit size, but cooperation between neighboring residents could result in larger or smaller units. Drawing upon initial research, the standard unit would offer a substantial size increase compared with those typically found in Central Havana while still being relatively compact. By offering a firm structural and infrastructural foundation yet allowing for residents to continue the culture of self-made housing, this project reflects the diversity and vibrancy of life in Central Havana.

01

(01) Intended as an in-fill strategy that could be deployed on multiple sites in Central Havana, this instance of the Havana Dom-ino is located on the eastern side of Galiano Street at the northern corner of the block.

UNDERSTANDING CUBAN SPACE

Average square footage per houshold

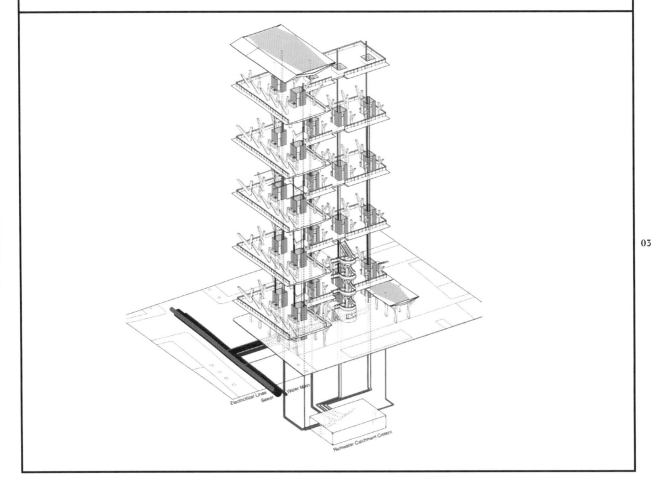

United States 2012 ...	2,400 sqft for 2.6 people
Australia ...	2,217 sqft for 2.3 people
United States 1973 ...	1660 sqft for 2.3 people
Denmark ...	1475 sqft for 2.2 people
France ...	1216 sqft for 1.5 people
Spain ...	1044 sqft for 2.7 people
Ireland / Havana ...	947 sq ft for 3.1 people / 939 sqftr for 3.57 people
United Kingdom ...	818 sqft for 2.27 people
Havana Domino ...	576 sq ft for 3.5 people
Central Havana ...	284 sqft for 3.57 people

Average square footage per person

Austrailia and US 2010

Denmark and US 1973

France

Spain and United Kingdom

Ireland and Havava

Havana Domino

Central Havana

02

03

(02) Early research and analysis focused on the typical allocation of space per person in Central Havana. The amount of space per household in Havana is roughly equivalent to the amount of space per person in the U.S. and Australia. Moreover, the amount of space per household in Central Havana is roughly equivalent to the amount of space per person in the rest of Havana. (03) Service cores supply the building with municipal water, electricity, and access to sewage lines as well as water from the rainwater catchment system.

Galiano: Colon and Guadalupe Districts

The Colon and Guadalupe districts flank opposite sides of Galiano Street. The former is among the densest sectors in Central Havana, while the Guadalupe District is also known as Chinatown. Studio projects sited within these districts varied in size and scope and strove to understand the extreme conditions of the substandard contemporary dwelling unit in Central Havana as a means to define the idea of a contemporary housing unit for the city.

Alexander Chabla & Edward Hsu— Micro Havana

This project's site is located in the heart of Havana, along Galiano Street. Now a derelict park, the site is situated within a dense urban fabric of terraced buildings. The striated grain of this fabric is drawn across the site as an organizational strategy and reflected in the building's longitudinal orientation. An intense and comprehensive study of current housing conditions was undertaken while visiting Havana. By meeting Habaneros, or citizens of Havana, and being invited into their homes, a deep understanding of the current standard of housing in Central Havana was obtained. Measurements and living arrangements were recorded and compiled, and they informed the project.

Taking into account the realities of housing in Central Havana, the project is set back from the street to provide space for a plaza, which acts as a place for pause and as a threshold between the district's relentless thoroughfares and the proposed housing units. This plaza preserves the relief that is currently offered by the park. The building is embedded within the urban fabric while maintaining a recognizable public front. The ground floor is perceived as a transparent public zone, revealing the activity within and establishing the building's presence as a space of urban relief within the district. The facade uses a brise-soleil system to provide shelter from Havana's summer heat and aspires to blend into the rhythm of the city's colonnaded streets.

The longitudinal strips of public space, which are woven between the housing units, blend at points of adjacency and create courtyards. These interior courtyards provide quiet moments within the building that offer the dwellers an escape from the city. The units themselves reflect the insights that were obtained through the studio's observations of current living conditions. The creativity and resourcefulness of the Habaneros in making the most of what little space they have is fostered by planning for overlapping functions within the units.

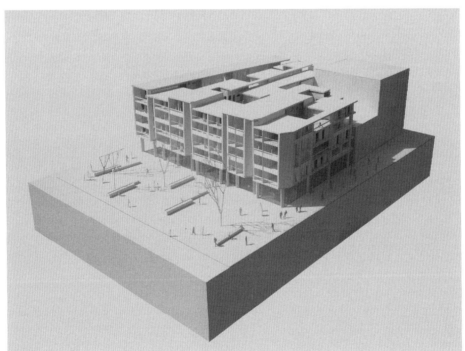

01

(01) The building facade along Galiano Street and the park is populated by housing units and their respective balconies. The balconies offer shade as well as an opportunity for residents to engage in the life of the street.

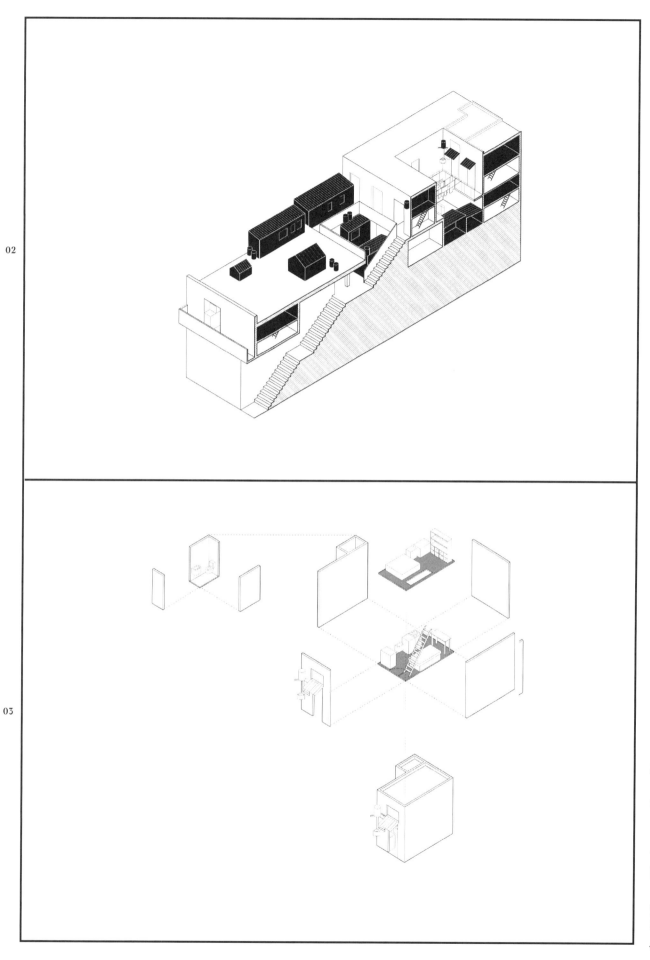

02

03

(02) The larger building in which the surveyed barbacoa is situated contains multiple user-built interventions. Called out in black, housing and additional levels within the overall structure have been built by residents. (03) This exploded axonometric diagram shows the contingent parts of the surveyed barbacoa. The second level of the unit is owner-built.

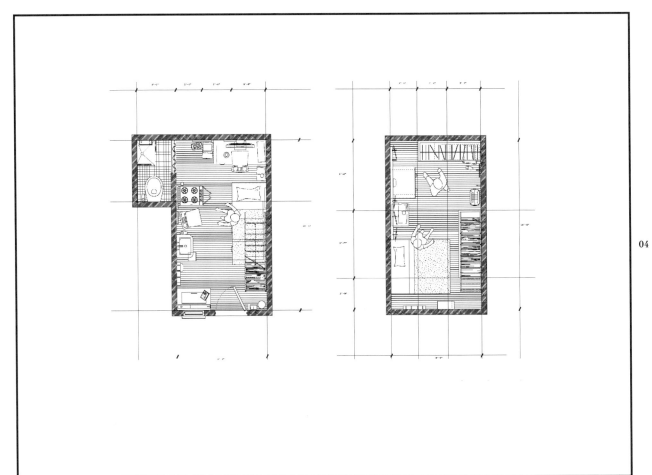

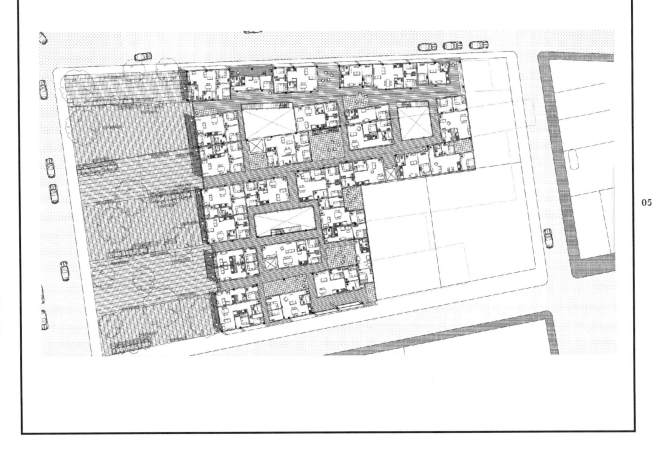

05

(04) Surveyed on site, this example of a barbacoa shows the incredibly tight conditions in a unit that houses three residents. In order to live in these conditions, every inch of space must serve multiple functions. (05) The second-level plan shows a typical residential floor of the project. Units front onto the public corridors, and three larger court-yards allow light and air into the interior of the lot. The building's grid continues into the park through the arrangement of landscaping and paving.

(06) Rendering of a typical public corridor in the proposal. As in the barbacoas, seemingly utilitarian spaces, such as corridors, can be used for multiple purposes, such as public gatherings and recreation.

06

Mansi Maheshwari—Public Space on Galiano

This proposal, located in the vibrant and busy center of Havana, intends to create a new public space by introducing into the urban fabric a void, which is as much a part of the life and activity of the streets as it is a relief from it. There are three distinct usage zones in the proposal: public activity, semi-public community functions, and private housing. These spaces are vertically layered in distinct yet interconnected sections of the building.

The ground floor is carved out of the surrounding city as a space devoid of a fixed program, allowing the dense activities of the street to spill into it. A series of columns gives structure to this hypostyle hall and creates a rhythm that suggests an organizational strategy for vendors and carts during a temporary market setup. The hypostyle hall could function as a fruit market, a space for music performances and street theater, coffee and cigar stores, or simply act as a covered public space offering relief from Cuba's hot sun. The second floor is an intermediary layer between the lower public realm and the upper private housing; it functions as a community space that may be rented out by small businesses or used as an after-school music institute, depending on the needs of the neighborhood. The private housing floors begin thirty-five feet above the street and are designed to foster maximum air circulation and ventilation. The units are planned around a central courtyard, the circulation around which extends out to the streets. The entrance of each housing unit is expressed by a thickening of the circulation that not only articulates the threshold but also provides space for residents to put up planters, curios, and nameplates. Service zones are planned in the central bays of the floor plates and allow flexible layouts for one- and two-bedroom units.

01

(01) View from one of the interior housing corridors. The corridors offer a visual connection to the street while preserving an amount of privacy and quiet. A large central courtyard allows light and air to enter the block.

02

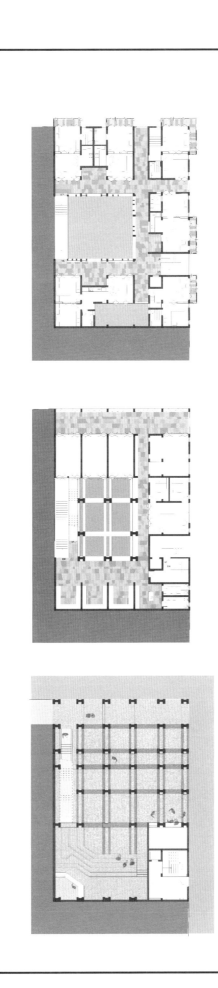

(02) The ground-floor plan shows the open hypostyle hall as well as the continuation of the Galiano Street arcade. The second-floor plan shows the transitional level of spaces available for community uses. The typical residential floor plan shows the central courtyard around which the circulation corridors are arranged. Units front onto the streets and have balconies for semi-outdoor living above the street level.

03

04

(03) View from inside the hypostyle hall, looking out toward Galiano Street. The open space can be used for functions such as markets or public gatherings and creates an extension of the continuous arcade along Galiano Street. (04) View of the proposal from across Galiano Street in the existing public park. Housing units face onto the street above the open hypostyle hall.

Galiano: Punta and Monserrate Districts

The Punta and Monserrate districts flank opposite sides of Galiano Street, defining its northernmost edges as the street intersects the Malecon and Havana's broad waterfront promenade and seawall. Prior to the construction of this esplanade, these districts defined the waterfront elevation of the city. Projects in this sector explored the design of new housing typologies, capable of capitalizing on the prominent views of the sea beyond.

Lauren Page—Artist (in) Residence

This proposal creates a new typology within Central Havana, weaving together both public and private programs to create flexible residential and artist studio spaces within the framework of a vertical public gallery. The merging of housing, artist studios, and gallery space creates a live-work condition that can allow for minimizing the size of private residential units in exchange for providing large communal studio spaces. In recent years, artists have been forced to look outside the center of the city to find adequate studio space. The creation of studio spaces within Central Havana serves to draw artists back into this area of the city where the density is typically too high to allow for workspaces.

The project opens up the typically solid street front by connecting the Galiano Street arcade to an interior, open public space in which the resident artists and the general public can interact. The gallery also engages the public street corner by presenting ribbons of balconies that thread vertically through the massing. These balconies generate flexible exterior spaces that are expressed on the Galiano Street facade. Anchoring the courtyard building at the corner with a tall studio tower, the project responds to the standard Galiano Street massing typology—a condition in which tall buildings are typically located on the corners of blocks. The lower register of the project is calibrated to the rhythm of the adjacent, lower buildings and is arranged to allow sunlight into the courtyard. The balconies are composed of a bright material whose appearance changes with age and contrasts with the monolithic concrete studio tower. This approach creates a system of color and texture that can be perceived when residents weave in and out of the building massing.

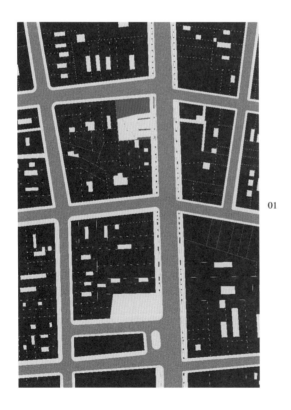

01

(01) The site plan shows the location of the proposal on a corner lot on the west side of Galiano Street. The arcade is continued along the front facade and connected to the central courtyard.

02

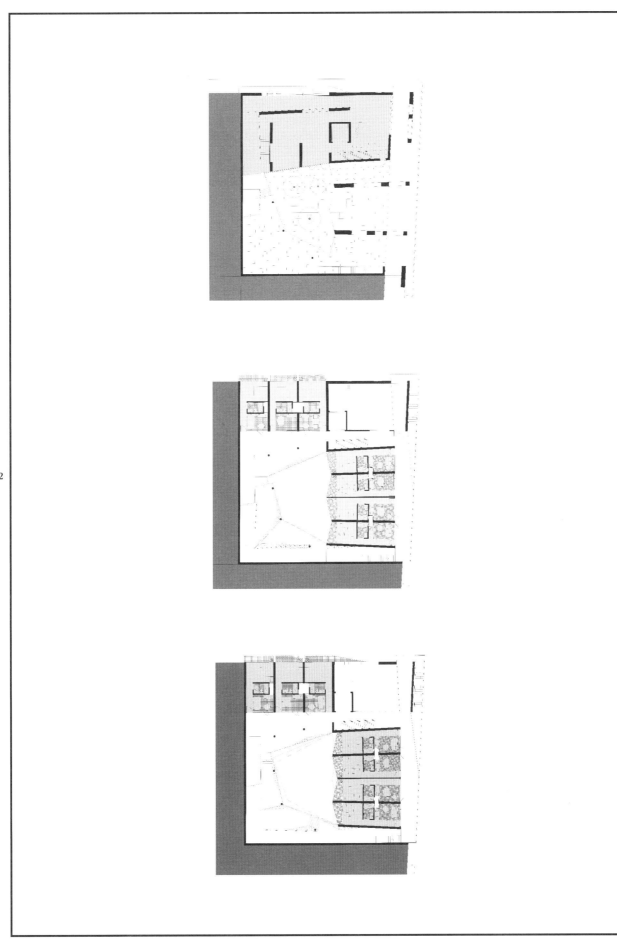

(02) The ground-floor plan shows the central courtyard and its connection to Galiano Street. The building lobby occupies the corner at the
base of the tower. The second-floor plan shows one of two typical plan
arrangements. Each unit provides living and studio spaces. The studio
spaces open onto the central courtyard. The third-floor plan shows the
second typical plan arrangement. Exterior balconies are strung along
the Animas Street facade.

Lauren Page—Artist (in) Residence

03

(03) A view of the central courtyard, looking up toward the corner tower. Interior balconies project in alternating patterns to allow light to fall on them at all levels. Residents' work can be executed and displayed outdoors on these balconies.

Alexander Osei-Bonsu—Incremental Housing in Central Havana

Of particular interest in Central Havana is the way in which residents modify their own space. By virtue of their unofficial living situations, the populace has co-opted what space it can find and turned it into a home for their families. Incredible ingenuity and resourcefulness in the use of space can be seen throughout the city. In this proposal, incremental housing is not only accounted for but specifically encouraged. By offering Habaneros a basic framework in which to work, they may continue their current tradition of agency and affecting their own environment.

The intersection of Galiano and Animas Streets creates an important biaxial dynamic for this site. Both the north-facing and east-facing facades are treated similarly, with apertures in the facade present only for public balcony space. Richness in the facade is largely introduced by the organized chaos of the contingent, built-out unit. In the most extreme manifestations, each unit would be built in different materials and colors, in turn reflecting the richness and diversity of the surrounding buildings. The shifts in plane of the facade are negated by a standard, white prefabricated treatment that is juxtaposed against colorful, built-out spaces. The scale of the units is also tempered by the shifting of massing, color, and depth. Structural spans are an average of thirty-five feet, which offers ample sunlight in the units during daylight hours while accommodating the need for shade.

01

(01) View of the corner of Galiano and Animas streets. Shifts in the plane of the building massing create balcony spaces for the individual units, which can be enclosed as an extension of the unit. The anticipated variety in each unit's expression is tempered by the stark white exterior of the overall proposal.

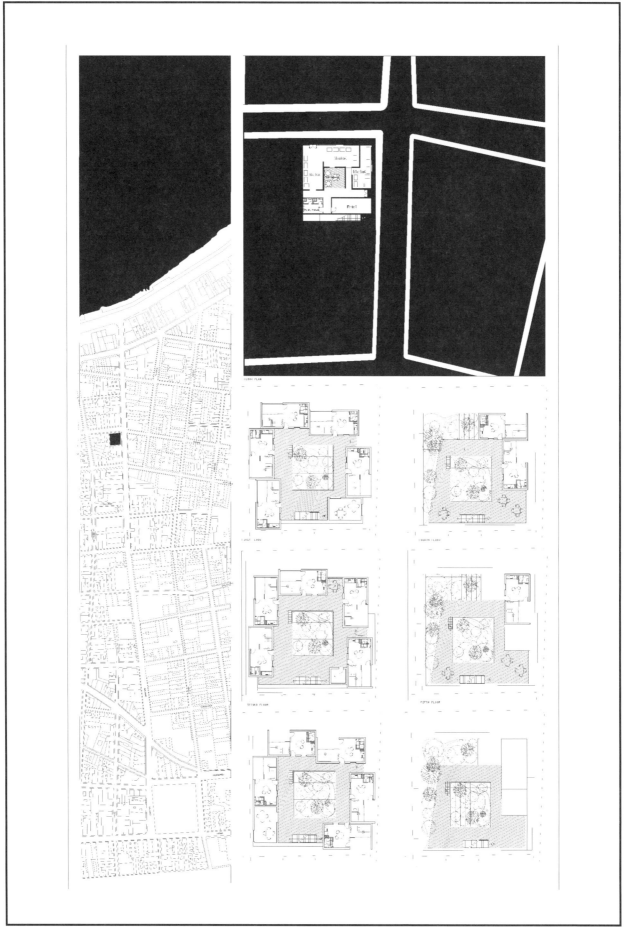

(02) The proposal is located on a corner site, near the water. The housing units are arranged around a central courtyard. Each unit has access
to ventilation for cooling.

Jeongyeap Shin—Vacant City and Expansion within Context

"No city can be saved unless it is loved. It can be cherished from afar and helped from afar, but it can be preserved only by people who love it from inside."
—Anthony Tung (former commissioner of the New York City Landmarks Preservation Commission)

There are three key issues that have influenced the current state of Central Havana. First, due to a decentralized development policy, the government controls all housing projects in Central Havana. Second, architecture in Cuba has been stymied, as the government banned private architectural practice in 1963 and protected the many historic buildings for the sake of tourism. These two outcomes have caused the proliferation of both vacant lots and buildings that retain only their original facades. Third, despite the fact that the construction of housing projects stopped in 1960, the population has increased 50 percent since then. Due to the limited amount of housing available, the average space allotted to each person continues to get smaller

and is currently even smaller than the government's recommendation.

With these issues in mind, a possible solution is expansion within the existing context. Employing an existing vacant building, specifically its facade, this proposal creates a strong relationship between the original building and the new expansion. The building reflects its Cuban context through its spatial quality, the treatment of the elevation, its physical dimensions, and the building materials used. At the ground level, a new library is introduced which can be enjoyed by the public and entered through the primary large opening in the existing facade. Above this, a central semi-public courtyard is open to the sky and contains the circulation for the housing units. Repeated above the courtyard, offset balconies provide more light and air circulation to the lower levels. As suggested in this proposal, the city can be saved only by maintaining its residents' inherited values.

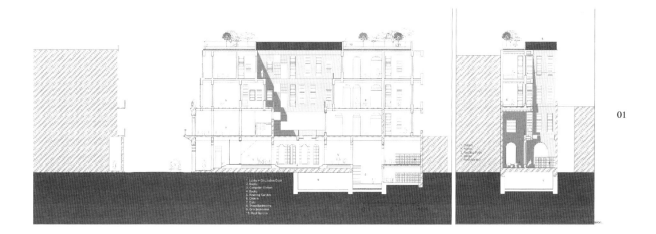

01

(01) Sections through the proposal show the central courtyard and the many different functions housed within the building. A library, café, reading patio, and housing units are all arranged around and below the courtyard.

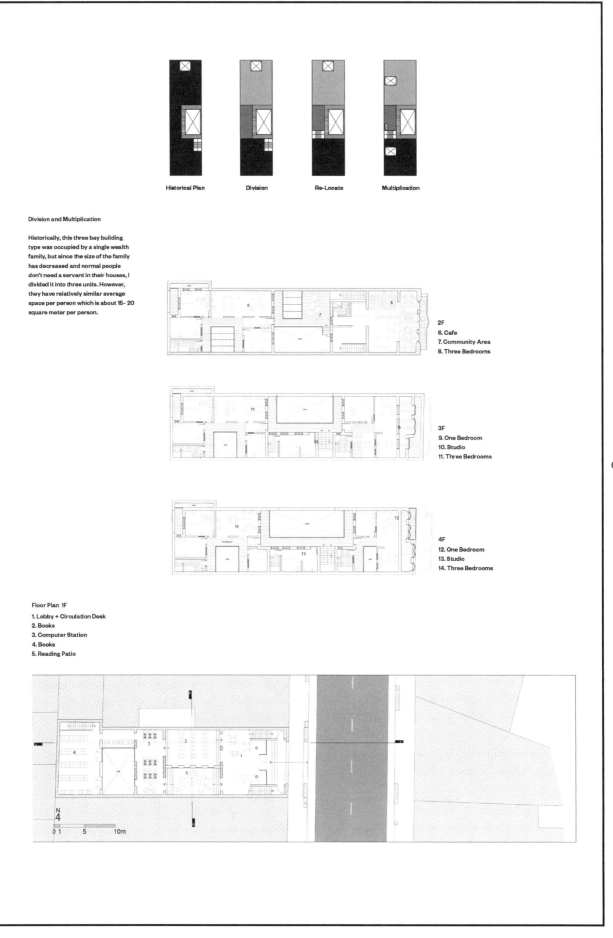

Historical Plan   Division   Re-Locate   Multiplication

Division and Multiplication

Historically, this three bay building type was occupied by a single wealth family, but since the size of the family has decreased and normal people don't need a servant in their houses, I divided it into three units. However, they have relatively similar average space per person which is about 15-20 square meter per person.

2F
6. Cafe
7. Community Area
8. Three Bedrooms

3F
9. One Bedroom
10. Studio
11. Three Bedrooms

4F
12. One Bedroom
13. Studio
14. Three Bedrooms

Floor Plan 1F
1. Lobby + Circulation Desk
2. Books
3. Computer Station
4. Books
5. Reading Patio

N
0 1   5   10m

(02) The ground-level plan shows the disposition of the library and reading patio. These elements open out to Galiano Street through the preserved historic facade and its large, theater like opening. The book stacks occupy the spaces to the rear of the lot, which do not receive much sunlight. Diagrams show the dual strategies for the division of units and multiplication of open spaces before the final plan arrangement.

Jeffrey Pollack—Casa de la Brisa

The future of Havana may include the loosening of government control, which could bring new investment and development to the historic districts of the city. As is typical of many historic city centers, the existing grain does not accommodate contemporary development standards. Central Havana consists mostly of thin lots that pose challenges for new housing. Rather than capitulate to the often detrimental concept of merging multiple lots, this proposal challenges the current building codes in order to preserve the existing grain of Central Havana while exploring modern housing types. Following the current code regulations on this typically small lot, maximum buildout affords a building with units at minimum square footages and no provision for outdoor space. As an alternative, this proposal's ten-story tower challenges the code-mandated five-story height limit and provides relatively large units, with 17 percent of the building reserved for public and private outdoor space.

Two aspects of working in Havana drive the design: taking advantage of the presence of highly skilled local craftsmen and finding a way to build appropriately for the tropical climate. Government-supported restoration efforts have nurtured a strong pool of workers skilled in building crafts and the use of traditional materials such as tile, stone, and wood. The building's materials are chosen based on this reality. A concrete frame, clad in tile to resist the corrosive sea air, is filled with operable wooden louvers and screens that can be replaced as needed. Caribbean examples of intelligent climatic design exhibit lightness, transparency, envelope permeability, and the judicious use of shade. Applying these lessons to the tower form, this proposal employs a shifted sectional diagram, which promotes cooling by increasing the amount of building envelope while shading the private patios. Plenum spaces on each floor naturally vent rising hot air, while a roof canopy and louvers shield the interior from the sun.

01

(01) View of the proposal in the context of the larger studio site model. Tall buildings are more common along Galiano Street as it approaches the Malecon and the water. The upper level is reserved as public space, which offers the residents views of Vedado and the coastline.

Jeffrey Pollack—Casa de la Brisa

02

(02) Sections of the proposal show the shifted floor-plate diagram.
By alternating the location of the open patios, the surface area of the
building skin is increased, allowing for enhanced passive cooling.
This strategy also ensures that each patio is shaded by the unit above.
Tall ceiling heights foster the extraction of warm air, and a large can-
opy at the top of the building shades the public roof terrace.

(03) View of the proposal from across Galiano Street. The upper residential floors are cantilevered over the sidewalk, continuing the shelter of the ground-level arcade at the street. Each three-bedroom housing unit occupies one floor and has its own outdoor patio space, which is shaded by sliding wooden screens.

03

Image Credits

Taiyo Watanabe: 11, 12, 15, 16, 17,
18, 19, 20, 21; Deegan Day Design:
13; Joe Day: 23, 25; Tom Wiscombe
Architecture: 77, 78, 79, 80, 81, 83,
84; Steven Brooke: 118, 120; Cúre
& Penabad: 119; Google Maps: 121;
Katharine Storr: 122 top, bottom
right, 123 bottom; Jeffrey Pollack:
122 bottom left, 123 middle; Antonia
Devine: 123 top, 130; Lauren
Page: 124 top; Mansi Maheshwari
& Jeongyeap Shin: 124 bottom;
Alexander Chabla & Edward Hsu:
125; Cúre & Penabad Studio: 126;
Antonia Devine & Christina Argyros:
127, 128.